THE WEDDI

HANDBOOK

MICHAEL J MACMAHON

Book 2 of the TELLING EXPERIENCE series

TABLE OF CONTENTS

FOREWORD

There are many things that are special about a wedding, especially for the two central protagonists (I phrase it that way because we can no longer assume that a wedding features a bride and groom). One thing it's easy to forget is that, unless the guest list is very small indeed, when you look afterwards at a photograph of all the guests, you're almost certainly seeing the only occasion in all of their lives when all of those people were together at the same time. (And they almost certainly *won't* all be there, because one or two are guaranteed to have nipped out for a smoke.)

Something else it's easy to forget is that some of the cast have to make speeches, and they may find that intimidating. And that applies whether they are experienced speakers or complete beginners. My daughter got married very recently, and I read this book with care beforehand because I was expected – as the father of the bride – to make a speech. As it happens, I've done a lot of speaking in public, but that didn't make me any the less nervous. My daughter depended on me. A whole bunch of people I'd never seen before also depended on me – in their case, not to bore them. I had to say the necessary things, I had to say them briefly and I had to say them well.

And that's all very well, but how do you do that? We get no practice. How many weddings have you been to? At how many of them did you have to speak?

The great majority of us attend weddings fairly rarely and almost never have a speaking part. (No, I'm not counting 'I do.') And so we have no practice in this very important part of the wedding ceremony. I hadn't, and the chances are that you haven't. Fortunately, Michael James MacMahon has provided a very knowledgeable guide for those called on to speak at a wedding.

I certainly needed it. Chances are you do, too.

John Lynch, author and entrepreneur

INTRODUCTION

The ability to express ourselves clearly and persuasively is of immense value in so many situations. But the prospect of doing just that while standing in front of a live audience terrifies most of us. For years psychologists have told us that public speaking is the number one phobia for a significant proportion of people.

I used to run training courses in organisations and one of our specialties was presentation skills. Over the years, therefore, I have trained many people who needed to make presentations in connection with their work. Sometimes they were inexperienced and sometimes they were regular speakers but wanted to polish their skills.

Speaking at a wedding is different. For a start, it might be an unfamiliar experience, because many wedding speakers have never spoken in public before. Even if you're used to public speaking, this is a very special and emotional occasion, particularly for the groom and for the father of the bride.

The best man (or woman) has an extra challenge. In our culture, he or she is expected to be funny, and that doesn't come naturally to everyone.

Yes, public speaking is recognised to be stressful for most people. The above factors, unique to weddings, add to the anxiety of the occasion. The speeches are not the *most* important part of the day but they are certainly important in our culture.

Given all this, what can you do to control this stress and get yourself into a positive and resourceful state of mind? Even if you're one of the lucky few who don't feel that stress, how can you plan your speech so it is the best it can be? A speech that all the guests – and, most importantly, the happy couple – will remember with pleasure.

WHAT PROMPTED ME TO WRITE THIS BOOK

I've been speaking in public for at least forty years. Nowadays I'm also a coach and one of my specialities is helping people to become better speakers.

Recently I've been asked to coach several people who had to speak at weddings. In the process I've discovered so many reasons why speaking at weddings can be even more stressful than speaking in public usually is.

Firstly, the speeches tend to be short, and that in itself requires more preparation. Winston Churchill used to say: 'If you want me to speak for twenty minutes, I need two weeks' warning. But if you want me to speak for two hours, I can begin now.' In other words, shorter speeches require more planning; and wedding speeches are usually much shorter than twenty minutes. (And they should be.)

Secondly and most importantly, I go back to the central fact that it's personal. It's a big day and it's a big deal. Especially for the father of the bride … and especially if this is the first time he's done this job. For the groom, it's (hopefully) the biggest day of his life so far. And for the best man, there is always that expectation of entertainment, although not all of us are natural entertainers.

Finally, there is a whole new category of wedding speakers, who previously had no voice in a British wedding: the mother of the bride, the bride herself and the maid of honour, or matron of honour, or chief bridesmaid. There may be a best woman too.

Today we also have same-sex weddings and it's now very common to have two or more best men. In different cultures in our diverse society, there are further variations on the customs relating to speakers. Whilst this book focuses on the customs that originated from a Christian culture and have also become relevant in secular weddings, I believe that much of the advice that I offer in this book will be equally relevant to those speaking at weddings in other cultures and other countries.

I have two wonderful daughters who have long-term partners. I always knew that if one of them should announce her engagement, I'd be nervous in advance. Those nerves are human, they are inevitable and, for reasons you will learn in this book, I would welcome them. What happened? Sure enough, while I was writing this book, one of those daughters got engaged. Then (I'm a slow writer) she got married. And the experience of speaking at her wedding proved to me the truth of the old saying 'it's what you learn after you know it all that counts.' I'll talk about that later.

We'll begin by discussing what you can do by way of long-term planning of your speech, well in advance of the day. We'll then talk about the practical things that can be done to cement into your subconscious the content you've planned. Finally, we'll deal with the things you can do ensure that your performance on the day is as good as it can be. Underpinning all that will be methods of managing those inevitable – but helpful – nerves.

DISCLAIMER: A REPETITION ALERT

Many readers (most readers, I imagine) will dip into this book to find the parts that apply to them. Thus it contains repetitions, for which I make no apology. That's because I want each chapter or section to be self-sufficient, not dependent on your having read a previous chapter or section. If you end up ignoring great chunks of the book because they don't apply to you, I promise not to be offended.

Chapter 1

Nervous? Why Fear Can Make You A Better Speaker

'There are only two types of speakers in the world: 1. The nervous; and 2. Liars.'

Mark Twain

Over the years I've become more and more convinced that a certain amount of nervous tension before any public performance is a helpful, maybe a necessary, ingredient of an optimum outcome. Maybe you agree with me already. If not, read on anyway. This chapter is all about those nerves, how they affect even the most celebrated performers, and how they can be managed in a practical way.

How do you feel about public speaking? For many people, it's the number one phobia in their lives. Most people even fear public speaking more than death, according to a survey reported in *The Times* in October 2013.

This kind of performance anxiety even affects those who are accomplished performers in what you'd consider related fields, including big-name actors you'll have heard of. The celebrated actor Dame Judi Dench was interviewed for the BBC Radio 4 programme *Desert Island Discs* in 2015. At the beginning of the programme, presenter Kirsty Young quoted something Dench had said about anxiety: 'Fear generates a huge energy. You can use it. When I feel that mounting fear, I think: "Oh yes, there it is!" It's like petrol.'

In the same interview Judi Dench elaborated on what she had said earlier, adding that the fear got worse with experience, because you recognise the pitfalls more. The interview also revealed that the world-famous and Oscar-winning Judi Dench fears public speaking far more than acting. So, if you too fear speaking in public – even if you're just a little bit anxious about it – you are not alone.

Your subconscious mind

When it comes to your wedding speech, your subconscious mind will be the number one driver of your performance on The Big Day. That subconscious, however, has a nasty habit of throwing up messages in a random way and they are usually negative ones. That's why mental preparation is so important.

It doesn't matter if the wedding is planned a year or two in advance, as many are, because the anxiety associated with the prospect of speaking will kick in as soon as you know where and when you're going to have to make the speech. My aim in writing this book is to help you with your preparation, so that the prospect of this speech doesn't become a mental sabre-toothed tiger every time the subject of the wedding comes up in conversation over the coming months; and it will.

Nervous? You're not alone. Lawrence Jackson's admission

How to get rid of your fears, or at least how to manage them, is 'the $64,000 question' in all public speaking. First of all though, there is an initial question: do you have fears? I have encountered eminent and experienced speakers who are never asked this question. Everyone makes the assumption that they don't have fears, because they have such experience and are so accomplished.

For many years I worked for big companies and in those days I went to lots of conferences. As a result I heard hundreds of speakers, good and bad. Just about the best after-dinner speaker I ever heard live was a man called Lawrence Jackson. He was a clergyman and his official title was Provost of Blackburn, but he was also a famous after-dinner speaker. When he retired, the then Bishop of the diocese declared that Jackson had 'put Blackburn on the map'; and when he died in 2002 his obituary in *The Daily Telegraph* included the following words:

... he was for many years the Church of England's premier entertainer. Jackson had all the gifts that would have ensured a successful career on the stage as a stand-up comic, had he not decided early in his life on taking Holy Orders. While the pulpit provided some outlet for this talent, his audiences were normally entertained in the hotels of Park Lane and other places of festivity where he was in great demand as an after-dinner speaker – he was on the books of one of the leading agencies.

Jackson was indeed fantastic. Normally I'd say that 20-25 minutes is enough for an after-dinner speech; but when I heard him, he spoke for over an hour and nobody wanted him to stop.

The event at which that happened was a residential conference. The following morning, when I went down to breakfast, I saw he was eating alone, so I asked if he'd mind if I joined him, as I was interested in his experiences as a speaker. He was very gracious and told me about his many speeches at high-profile dinners: for example in front of the Royal Family, at London's Mansion House, on TV etc.

Then I asked 'Is there any part of it you don't enjoy?'

'Yes: the reception before the dinner,' he replied.

'I can see that,' I said. 'You're sipping a drink and making small-talk to a total stranger whom you'll probably never meet again. But you're nervous because you're going to speak in an hour.'

'Thank you!' he answered. 'That's the first time for twenty years that anyone has suggested that I might be nervous. They assume that I'm not, because I do so much of this. But yes, I'm always nervous. And if I ever stop being nervous, I'll stop speaking.'

Inevitable … but manageable?

So most people, even the eminent ones I mentioned, have nerves in advance; they have nerves which create a sense of excitement. Perhaps fear is the wrong word here, but they have an adrenalin rush that, provided it's controlled, can deliver an extra boost of energy that drives the speech.

Here's the way I think of it when I'm speaking: that extra boost of energy – 'like petrol', as Dame Judi Dench said – enables my brain to be slightly ahead of my tongue, so that by the time I finish this sentence I know what I'm going to say next.

I said 'provided it's controlled' – but how do we do that? The important thing is that if you have fears – in other words, if you have negative expectations of the outcome of this forthcoming event – the trick is to replace those negative expectations with positive expectations. It is said that the conscious mind can only hold one thought at a time. However, the subconscious throws up little messages, little prompts, in a random way. When you know in advance you're going to have to speak in public, or do anything that is for you a stressful event, your subconscious can throw up the possibility of failure at times when you don't expect it. This often happens whenever the forthcoming event is mentioned by somebody else.

The reason this happens is interesting, and I'll come onto that later. More interesting, however, is learning what to do about it.

Now for the good news

The good news is that there are many techniques and tools that you can use to manage your mental state. I'll describe three of them here.

The more mental preparation that you do, the better you will manage your anxiety. As we've established, a certain amount of adrenalin on the day is almost inevitable and will give you the energy to drive your speech, but in order to control it you need this mental preparation.

The first element of this approach is talking to yourself about the upcoming occasion. A famous exponent of 'self-talk' was the legendary boxer Muhammad Ali. At his peak in the 1960s and '70s he was one of the most famous people on the planet; the BBC named him 'Sports Personality of the Century'. Ali used what are sometimes called affirmations. He went around saying, 'I am the greatest' for years, even before he became a champion. He said this to himself – and to anyone else who was around – so often that eventually he believed it. In later life he even joked about it: 'Yes, I said I was the greatest, even before I knew I was.'

So talking to yourself about the outcome of this event is one way of doing it, and it's used by a lot of people.

A further part of Ali's method – in fact the essential part, in my view – is visualizing the outcome. Maybe you have read about this. He called it his 'future history'. He would visualize the upcoming event, and the outcome that he wanted, in technicolour. I'll get to this technique in a minute. But first …

Back to basics: control your breathing, control your nerves

I am a keen rugby fan. In my playing days I was never a kicker, but I did and do recognise the extra pressures on those guys. Very often, the result of a match hangs on their successes or failures and each kick is a one-off event. Ever since England's legendary and World Cup-winning Jonny Wilkinson – and maybe before him but I didn't notice – kickers in the professional era have developed lengthy and elaborate preparation rituals.

During the latest Rugby World Cup I was particularly struck by something a commentator said, while a kicker was lining up an important penalty attempt. The commentator said: 'He'll be controlling his breathing before he starts his run-up,' or words to that effect. That was an obvious thing that I'd overlooked and which is relevant to any form of performance anxiety.

It reminded me that in my thirties I got involved in amateur drama, or 'am-dram' as we call it here. My father had been a very good actor in his thirties and forties and so, before my first-ever play, I asked him about last-minute rituals.

His reply was not what I expected but was brief and practical: 'While you're standing in the wings before your first entrance, check your flies and take three deep breaths.'

It's pretty clear that controlling your breathing is important. We sometimes forget that the natural tendency when nervous or stressed is to breathe quickly and shallowly, which is the opposite of what we need for delivering a good speech. So … if you can control your breathing, you've made a start at controlling your nerves.

Why is our subconscious mind so active at throwing up negative images?

It's always been my belief that positive expectations of an outcome are more likely to produce a positive outcome … provided I have an influence on that outcome, as is surely the case here. However, for many of us negative memories and negative expectations dominate in the deep recesses of our subconscious minds.

I love a quotation from the film director Baz Luhrmann, which came as part of a so-called commencement address he gave some years ago. His words were these:

'Remember the compliments you receive. Forget the insults.'

Luhrmann then added: 'If you can do this, please tell me how.'

What he is saying is that we are more likely to remember ways in which we have been offended or hurt in the past than to remember good things which people have said about us or done to us.

Past failures and negative expectations: Ken Wydro's speech

One could extend Baz Luhrmann's quotation to saying that we are also more likely to remember the mistakes we made, or the stupid things we said, than to remember our successes – and that can influence our expectations of the future. I will never forget the following experience, which illustrates the point perfectly.

Many years ago when I was at an industrial conference in the United States, I heard a superb talk by a speaker called Ken Wydro. He was a trainer and consultant in communication skills and his subject was Productivity under Pressure. (He's also an author, a playwright and theatre producer; a man of many talents). I knew that it was common in the States for conference organisers to book at least one motivational speaker who has no connection with the industry; Ken Wydro was one such speaker.

He began his talk by telling a story. He said, 'When I was at high school, I was unathletic and overweight. I was not a sporty person. This was a great disappointment to my father, who had been a sports star at that same school. However, my father persuaded the football coach to let me play in one of the games.' (For British readers, I should point out that this was American football and in that sport a player can be brought on for just one play, which might last five seconds or less.)

Wydro continued, 'So I put on all the equipment and ran out onto the field. The quarterback told me what I had to do. I had to run a few yards to the right and then a few yards back to the left, so as to end up just five yards in front of the quarterback, who would then throw me an easy pass. Guess what happened? In my one and only opportunity on the team, I dropped the ball.'

In a hall full of several hundred people, there was total silence. You could have heard a pin drop. Then Wydro continued, 'That was forty years ago; but since then, not a day has passed when I have not thought about it.'

The silence told a story in itself: everyone there had had a similar experience of something that went wrong – not necessarily about sport, not necessarily about school-days

– and it had left a scar.

The message was clear and Ken Wydro expanded on it with passion: how to control the tendency of our subconscious minds to throw up negative memories, which in turn can create negative expectations of the things we are doing today and tomorrow.

OK, I said we would get on to Ali's visualisation method and here it is.

THREE STRATEGIES FOR MANAGING NERVES

Creating positive expectations: Muhammad Ali and 'future history'

Whether or not evolutionary hard-wiring is the most important reason it exists, my aim is to propose strategies that might help you counteract our tendency to expect the worst.

So, going back to Muhammad Ali … whenever he attended a press conference to announce a fight for which he was contracted, immediately after the press conference was over he would excuse himself, go up to his hotel suite, draw the blinds, and just sit down and relax, breathe deeply and then create a picture of the fight.

More than just creating a picture: he even used to get into the detail of predicting in which round he was going to win. Ali would create this picture of the end of the fight, with his opponent flat on his back. He would then freeze-frame the picture and carry it around for the next two or three months, until the day of the fight. That was his version of what is sometimes called creative visualization; Ali called it 'future history'.

How could that method be tailored to your needs, to help you when you prepare for your wedding speech? What is your equivalent of that knockout moment? This is where you go back and remember your purpose in giving the speech; then you can create your own picture of a successful outcome. By your own definition, nobody else's. You might, for example, picture the smiling bride appreciating what you have said, or an enthusiastically applauding audience. That type of mental picture can help you anticipate the day ahead with pleasure rather than dread, so the techniques I'll outline will help you to focus on these new positive mental images.

The groom using Muhammad Ali's 'future history' method to visualise his speech

'The circle of excellence'

The second method I'd like to introduce to you – not so different from Ali's – is one that I've found extremely useful in my own speaking career. I learned about it when a friend and I attended a seminar about managing stress, run by an excellent British company called Brilliant Minds. The presenters began by saying that they could teach us how to eliminate the effect of nerves in advance of an important event. It so happened that the friend sitting next to me was an actor, like me, and she interjected, 'I'm sure Michael and I would both say that we need the adrenalin in order to give our best performance.'

One of the presenters replied, 'OK, I hear that. But I can show you a tool that enables you to manage the nerves, not remove them. Is one of you prepared to be a guinea-pig?'

I volunteered; and the presenter asked, 'When will you next be acting or speaking?'

I said, 'As it happens, I'll be speaking this evening at a fundraising dinner.'

'Can you see this circle on the ground?' she said (it was an imaginary circle, folks). 'Please step into the circle, close your eyes and cast your mind back to a time in the past when you were in the frame of mind in which you want to be this evening.' In my case, I wanted to feel calm but resourceful and full of energy.

I remembered that for more than ten years I'd hosted an annual conference at Heathrow for several hundred clients. It was a two-day or three-day event and I always gave the keynote address at the start. It always went well – except for one occasion that I'll mention later – and I felt really good while doing it. That was the feeling I wanted to remember, the state I wanted to re-create.

When I had done that, the trainer asked the other participants if they saw any change in my body language; they all said yes. In fact some of them laughed, because the change was so obvious.

She then asked me to make a little physical signal to myself, which I could use to call up this feeling again. I chose to squeeze together the thumb and ring finger of my right hand. Next, she asked me to come back to the present moment, open my eyes and step out of the imaginary circle. When I had done that she picked up the imaginary circle, scrunched it up together as if it were a collapsible hula-hoop, and told me to put in my pocket.

'When you get home this evening,' she suggested, 'put the circle down on the floor, step into the circle and make the sign to yourself, so as to repeat the process in reverse.'

I did that and the effect was remarkable. That evening, on the way to the dinner at the Marriott Royal Hotel in Bristol, where I was speaking at a fundraising dinner organised by Airbus, I phoned the trainer to tell her how exceptionally good the tool had been. When I arrived at the venue, the difference was even more palpable. The speech went fine, as I'd expected, but the difference was that I felt so relaxed in the time leading up to it – in other words while talking to people at the reception and during the meal – that I was able to pick up some new information and insights which I could then add to my speech. Previously, I would never do that at the last moment: I'd prepare, get myself in the zone and create a mental bubble around myself.

In over 40 years of public speaking, it was one of the best performances I had ever given and I ascribe its success to discovering this technique, which is sometimes called 'anchoring' and sometimes called 'the circle of excellence'. It is part of the toolkit of NLP (neurolinguistic programming) practitioners.

The 'safe place' method

The third technique was described to me by a dear friend who's a retired teacher. Many years ago, her colleagues were feeling stressed out by a forthcoming visit by OFSTED, the dreaded school inspectors we have here in the UK. So the enlightened head teacher at her school taught the staff a method that would enable anyone to enter a relaxed state with ease: by finding somewhere quiet, sitting down, breathing deeply, and then visualising a favourite place. It could be somewhere they liked to visit on holiday, for example: anywhere that made them feel calm and contented by thinking of it.

From then onwards, whenever my friend or her colleagues felt stressed, instead of taking a cigarette break – this was some years ago, as I said, and at that time smoking was more widespread – they could 'take themselves off for a mental break', without ever having to leave the staff-room. I realise that a school staffroom was probably not the quietest place in the world, but the fact that my friend and her colleagues found this technique valuable speaks volumes. This method of relaxing is a priceless skill that we all can benefit from learning, teachers or not.

If you've ever worked in education you'll know that the stress can be extremely debilitating. The comedian and writer Jeremy Hardy had a newspaper column, in which he once wrote: 'Teaching is a branch of the performing arts. And a day in front of thirty kids is a bloody long gig.' Any technique that can help manage stress in teaching, where the pressures are almost continuous, can also work effectively for shorter periods of performance anxiety, such as preparing and delivering a speech.

Breaking news about stress

Recently published research coming from psychologists and other academics at Stanford University in California seems to reveal a fascinating fact about stress. It's long been said that excessive stress can be bad for one's health in many ways. But the research which is described in a fascinating book called *The Upside of Stress* (2015) by Dr Kelly McGonigal reveals that advice is now being modified as follows:

- A certain amount of stress is beneficial, if not essential (and we all know that what is stressful for Person A is a breeze for Person B)

- What's harmful is not stress in itself ... but the *belief* that stress is harmful

- People who have been conditioned by simple methods to accept and welcome stress (think of Judi Dench and 'there it is: I can use it') exhibit markedly fewer negative effects from a given stressful event.

If this theory becomes widely accepted, then it will totally change the way we can coach people to prepare for stressful events of all kinds. It will mean finding the most effective ways of changing a person's 'stress mindset'. The Stanford studies seem to show that this can be done easily and quickly.

When my stage performance went wrong … and why

I talked earlier about that conference I used to host. My keynote speech always went well because I had planned it and prepared for it. I used to get nervous of course but that helped. Let me tell you how I know that last fact.

The conference was mostly papers given by individuals but there were also some panel discussions, chaired by well-known people in the industry. One year, a chairman was taken ill and had to drop out at the last moment, so I had to chair one of the panel sessions. Because this happened at short notice, I didn't have time to get nervous.

It was a task that normally I'd have found very easy and could have dealt with OK. I had given my keynote speech a couple of hours before and it had gone particularly well. So I was very relaxed: no nerves at all.

What happened? I was rubbish. I know for a fact that I didn't do it well, because I was too relaxed. I wasn't on the ball, to use a sporting metaphor. To be precise, I didn't have the benefit of adrenalin helping me to think a couple of seconds ahead.

Why does our subconscious throw up the fear of possible failure so readily?

I said I would get onto this question. I find it interesting, though not as interesting as developing strategies for counteracting the tendency, but here it is anyway.

For years I've wondered why our subconscious mind seems to be so active in throwing up negative, rather than positive, pictures. One theory is evolutionary: our species has over the millennia become hard-wired for problem-solving and survival. Thus we are more likely to remember things that went wrong in the past, in order to work out ways to avoid negative outcomes next time. So the subconscious is more likely to throw up warnings of future risks than pictures of future successes.

As Russ Harris says in *The Happiness Trap*:

'Our minds did not evolve to make us feel good, or so we could tell jokes or write poems. Our minds evolved to keep us safe in a world of danger ... with each generation the human mind became increasingly skilled at predicting and avoiding danger ... constantly on the lookout, assessing everything we encounter: is this good or bad? Safe or dangerous? Harmful or helpful? These days, though, it's not sabre-toothed tigers ... it's about common worries. As a result we spend a lot of time worrying about things that, more often than not, never happen.'

Never happen? There's a famous quotation on the subject: 'My life has been full of terrible misfortunes, most of which never happened.' That was Michel de Montaigne, back in the sixteenth century. Mark Twain has said something similar more recently but I've quoted him already and he doesn't need any more exposure.

CHECKLIST

The techniques I have described here can work for you in relation to your wedding speech. However, in order to tackle your nerves, it's important to take action. If you don't practice the techniques, they will simply remain just words on a page.

For example, let's take Strategy 1, Muhammad Ali's 'future history' approach. Here's what I suggest:

❑ Get totally relaxed (preferably in a dark, quiet place) and conjure up the outcome you want. The bridesmaids falling about with laughter? The grumpiest person at the wedding nodding their approval? You choose.

❑ Ask yourself: what would this look like, feel like, sound like? Create a mental movie of that moment, then freeze-frame the picture. Come back to the present moment and then carry that 'future history' around with you until the Big Day.

Or you might like Strategy 2, the 'circle of excellence' approach. It's the reverse of 'future history', as it relies on remembering a past success.

❑ Decide what state of mind you want to be in on the big day. For example, full of energy? Calm? Fluent? Inspirational? Any or all of those?

❑ Remember a time in the past when you were in that state of mind.

❑ Picture a circle on the ground; step into it, close your eyes, relax and cast your mind back to that past time.

❑ Allow yourself time to recall all the memories in detail. How did you feel, what did you see, hear, smell etc.?

❑ When you are truly in that past moment, and feeling the emotions you felt then, give yourself a little physical sign. Some people squeeze an earlobe; I squeeze together the thumb and ring finger of my right hand: you choose your own signal or 'anchor'.

❑ Come back to the present moment: step out of the 'circle', scrunch it up and put it in your pocket or handbag.

❑ Whenever anxiety hits you, retrieve the 'circle', put it on the ground, step into it, reverse the process by giving yourself the signal you chose.

Finally, and also using memories of the past, there was Strategy 3, the 'safe place' method, which uses mental pictures of a place rather than an event.

❑ Find a quiet place, if possible.

❑ Sit or lie down in a comfortable position. Many people choose to lie flat on the floor with their palms facing up to the ceiling. You might want to place a paperback book beneath your head for support or to bend your knees and put your feet flat on the floor to support your lower back.

❑ Breathe deeply, focus on your breath, then focus on each part of your body relaxing, starting from your scalp and working down to your toes. Once you feel fully relaxed, create a mental picture of a favourite place.

❑ Choose a single word to represent that mental picture.

❑ Then that word can be used to take you in your head to that 'safe place' for mental refreshment whenever you feel stressed.

All of these techniques have worked for me at different times. This may seem an unusual place to begin planning for your wedding speech, but if you can master the ability to remain calm and relaxed, then the speech you will give on the day will inevitably come from a speaker who is confident and in control of their emotions: someone who may be a little nervous, but who is able to talk calmly and with ease, enabling all those listening to feel equally relaxed and to engage fully with what is being said and the emotion behind it.

Chapter 2

What's Expected of the Wedding Speaker

'My most brilliant achievement was my ability to persuade my wife to marry me.'

Winston Churchill

I'm a bit of a traditionalist when it comes to weddings. So in this chapter I talk about the traditions, or conventions, that have grown up in our culture around the speeches. I'll talk about the various people who'll be speaking and what could be expected from each of them by the audience. To what extent you want to follow these traditions is up to you; but first you need to know what they are.

A wedding is a momentous event. Whether it's in a church, a registry office or any other venue, it is a formal and public commitment by two people in front of family and friends. For that reason it is natural that conventions – or traditions, if you like – have grown up around the way it is organised.

As I'm a Brit, what I say about traditions refers to those in this country. And one of those traditions is this: whether the event as a whole is going to be formal or informal, the speeches are an important part of the day. Therefore, certain traditions, in turn, have grown up around those speeches.

To what extent you feel yourself bound by these traditions is, however, entirely up to you – specifically to the bride and groom, who set the tone of the event. In general, I like to question traditions, but a wedding is one situation where I personally would stick to them. That's me; it's not necessarily you. These days, more and more people are making their own rules and that's fine.

The speeches usually happen at the end of the meal – the wedding breakfast, as it used to be called. Here are the basics of what is expected of the main speeches, by tradition and in the usual order.

- The bride's father: welcoming the guests, proposing a toast to the bride and groom.

- The groom: responding on behalf of the couple, thanking those who've helped with the day, proposing a toast to the bridesmaids (or to the maid of honour or matron of honour).

- The best man, responding on behalf of the bridesmaids.

What's your role at this wedding?

For many years, the speeches at a wedding in the UK have been restricted to a cast of three: the father of the bride, the groom and the best man. However, in other cultures, and increasingly now in the UK, there can also be speeches by the bride, the mother of the bride, the chief bridesmaid / maid of honour / matron of honour, or by other relatives or friends. According to *Wedding Ideas* magazine: 'who says you can't have a best woman and a man of honour?'

Changing customs

As we've seen, in the British tradition the speeches all come at the end of the wedding meal. That is beginning to change, because some couples now prefer to spread them out: for example, one before the meal starts, one in the middle and one at the end. That's a change that has benefits both for the guests and the speakers, though it is less popular with catering staff. And it's a change I like, so I'll come back to that.

Each speech except that of the best man is traditionally ended by proposing a toast, although most best men end by repeating the toast given by the bride's father, i.e. to the bride and groom.

In some countries (particularly the US) the speeches themselves are called toasts; and they are usually (but not always) shorter and more informal than in the UK. Here, where formality has been our watchword for so many centuries, the word 'toast' refers only to the invitation at the end of the speech for the assembled company to join the speaker in drinking the health of someone.

So, in the British tradition, wedding speeches are usually made in this order:

i. The bride's father, who ends by proposing a toast to the bride and groom
ii. The groom, who ends by proposing a toast to the bridesmaids (or maid of honour or matron of honour)
iii. The best man, responding on behalf of the bridesmaids, who often finishes his speech by reading out any messages (they used to be

telegrams, if you can remember that far back) that have been received.

[In the above list, for 'bridesmaids' one could substitute 'maid of honour' or 'matron of honour'.]

It's increasingly common (even in our hidebound old country) for there to be a speech by the bride. There can also be speeches by a best woman, if there is one, or other relatives and friends. I was toastmaster at a big wedding in Norway and there were twelve speeches, of which half were by women; an example we might follow in the UK, eventually.

By the way, two of those speeches included a song; that's another thing I hope we will learn from our Nordic neighbours.

Who's involved?

The father of the bride

I include under this heading not only the bride's actual father but also, as it's increasingly common, her stepfather, or sometimes a brother. It's whoever 'gives her away', to use our quaint and somewhat anachronistic term. For second marriages, the role is sometimes taken by a son. In the past I once fulfilled this role myself for a neighbour's family. Whilst I wasn't a relation, I was 'giving the bride away', so I gave that first speech.

If you're in the 'father of the bride' role, then your primary tasks are threefold: to welcome the guests (in this context you speak as if you are the host, whether or not you are paying the costs of the wedding); then to tell everyone what a wonderful person the bride is (in case they didn't know) and to say something about the groom; and finally to propose a toast. Your toast will be 'the bride and groom'.

In the past, the bride's family was responsible for the entire cost of the wedding. However, more and more often nowadays the couple themselves pay part or all of the wedding costs, especially when one of them has been married before, or if they are financially well-placed to cover those costs. That doesn't change the fact that the father of the bride usually speaks first.

The groom

If you're the groom, you'll also begin your speech by thanking people.

Firstly you'll reply, on behalf of your bride and yourself, to the toast just proposed by the bride's father. And you'll thank him for the very positive things he has just said about you. At least I very much hope that he has. I remember that on my own wedding day, my new father-in-law most certainly did that, so I said I hoped I could live up to his compliments.

You might want to add and personalise some words of welcome to the guests, in addition to those already said by your bride's father. After all, you probably know them all, which he might not.

You'll probably want to thank those who have helped to organise the day, and those who have paid for it, if it wasn't you and your bride.

Naturally and most importantly, you will want to say something good about your new wife. Actually, something very good indeed about your wife: that would be my advice.

The traditional conclusion to the groom's speech is a toast to the bridesmaids in general, or to the chief bridesmaid, or matron of honour if she herself is married. These days there might be a maid of honour instead. Whatever she's called at your wedding, the bride's chief attendant is the person that the groom concludes by toasting. Although this is a tradition that is starting to die out, it is the tradition.

The best man

The formal demand on the best man at a British wedding is simple: to respond to the groom's final toast. If the convention has been followed, then you're responding on behalf of the bridesmaids in general, or the chief bridesmaid (or maid of honour) in particular. After that, the format is up to you.

You do not have to conclude with a toast, although many best men repeat the toast to the bride and groom.

Again: do remember that all the above are the traditions or conventions, which you can observe or ignore as you choose. What will matter most is how you personalise your speech and how you put it across with feeling, and we'll get to that. For now, we are simply focusing on 'what is expected' – but to make your speech stand out, you will learn in this book how to personalise it and make it come fully alive.

Other speakers ... the bride, the bride's mother, the maid of honour ...

Although our traditions in the past provided for just three speeches (all by men), more and more brides are now choosing to speak at their own weddings. About time too!

In other countries it has been different for some time. I once spoke at a fiftieth birthday party in Sweden (where that particular birthday is a very big deal) and more recently

I've been the toastmaster at a large wedding reception in Norway. At both of these events, there were lots of speakers (maybe a dozen each time) and half of them were women.

Now here's the good news for any female speaker at a wedding, or for any speaker apart from the three main ones … there are no traditions about what you should or should not say. It's simply a matter for your taste and your good sense.

Multiple best men

A recent redevelopment in the UK has been the practice for two or more friends of the groom to share the role of best man. One of my daughters, who attends lots of weddings, says she can't remember the last time there was only one best man. I've even heard of a wedding that had six.

In a way, this newer development replaces the previous custom of appointing a best man and two or three ushers. With ushers it was clear what their job was. With multiple best men, it's less clear. It's common for them to share the speechmaking duties, which is great … provided they coordinate their speeches. It's not so great for guests to hear the same stories and jokes repeated, if the best men have not taken the time to plan the content between them.

Length of speeches

At most weddings the speeches average between five and ten minutes each. It's common for the best man's speech to be the longest but ten minutes is generally enough there too. If there are two or three best men and they are all speaking, then five minutes each should be sufficient. Brevity is the soul of wit, as the saying goes.

This puts a pressure on the speakers to compress their material. A short speech, as I've already suggested, requires a lot of preparation.

A well-known website for public speakers (*Six Minutes*, hosted by Canadian Andrew Dlugan) analysed a series of televised talks (the famous *TED Talks*) by celebrities. Their average speed was 163 words / minute and the range was from 133 to 188.

If you're a Brit you might like to know that our very witty (well, I think so) educationalist Sir Ken Robinson spoke at 168 words / minute. And if you're American you'd like to know that the late Steve Jobs spoke at 158 but Al Gore at only 133. Clearly, we all speak at different speeds … but my advice would be to speak *at a slower speed than is normal for you*. The effect of adrenalin will speed everything up in your mind, so a pause that seems like five minutes to you will seem like two seconds to the audience.

So, for guidance while you're drafting your speech, if you plan to speak for five minutes that's only about 500–700 words, at the speed most people speak.

When are the speeches delivered? And why?

In our culture, speeches have always been at the end of the meal and that's not just at weddings but at other formal meals too. I can't think of a reason, except that (a) it makes it easier for the catering staff to plan the service and (b) 'that's the way we have always done it'. The result is that the speakers don't usually enjoy the food.

Moreover, being nervous those speakers could well be tempted to put away lots of wine while waiting to speak. That's understandable, but unwise if you want to give your best performance.

I am glad to see that this timing tradition is being challenged. Occasionally, these days, speeches are at the beginning of the meal and sometimes they are spaced out throughout it: one at the start or after the first course, one after the main course and one after coffee. It's a great idea, though it does require extra coordination with the catering staff.

I mentioned that one of my daughters did indeed get married. I was very pleased about the decision she and her groom made about the timing of speeches. They chose to time them between the starter and the main course. That was a modern trend I welcomed, traditionalist though I am about most wedding customs. I was the first to speak; and then I could do justice to the food … and the wine.

Those toasts!

I've mentioned that I am a coach. Occasionally I help people to write their speeches but what that means is that I show them how to do it themselves. I would never advise a client to use someone else's words for such an important occasion. Worst of all in my opinion is drafting a speech by means of cutting and pasting sample speeches, and especially jokes, from online sources. So I counsel my clients to find ways of avoiding that strategy.

There is however, one exception to my decision to avoid speech samples in this book. The toasts at the end of each speech are so standardised that I'll repeat them here and I'm very happy if you want to copy them verbatim.

By the way, in the US the speeches themselves are often called toasts, whereas here in the UK the word toast refers just to the formal phrase at the end of a speech, meaning 'please join me in drinking the health of …' That's another example of 'two nations divided by a common language', to quote George Bernard Shaw.

Father of the Bride: 'Finally, ladies and gentlemen, I'd like to propose a toast. Please charge your glasses (and pause if necessary for this important task to be completed) ... to be upstanding (pause) ... and to join me in drinking the health of X and Y ... (pause) ... the bride and groom!'

Groom: 'Finally, ladies and gentlemen, I ask you to charge your glasses (pause), to be upstanding (pause) ... and to join me in drinking the health of the bridesmaids!' or '... in drinking the health of the Maid of Honour (or Matron of Honour)' (in which case name her).

These days, the groom's toast to the bridesmaids or Maid of Honour is often forgotten or just omitted. That's a pity, in my view; but then I'm a traditionalist about these things. Many grooms improvise a different toast instead, for instance to their new bride or to 'friends and family.'

Best Man: no concluding toast is specified by our conventions. However, many best men repeat the father's toast to the bride and groom, which is of course a neat way of finishing the formal part of the proceedings.

If there are also speeches by the bride and /or her mother, or other family members or friends, they tend to do the same, i.e. to finish by repeating the toast to the bride and groom.

CHECKLIST

- ❏ Keep it short! Wedding speeches average five minutes. Don't go over ten unless you're amazingly talented.
- ❏ Bride's father: welcome guests. Finish by toasting the happy couple.

❏ Groom: thank everyone who has helped in connection with the day (and this is often the point at which gifts are presented to such people). Then it's all about your bride. Finish with the traditional toast to the bridesmaids in general – or the bride's chief attendant in particular – or improvise another toast.

❏ Best man: You're replying to the groom's toast. After that, it's up to you. Jokes are usually expected but not absolutely necessary. Personal stories are better, unless the jokes are fantastic (and new!) AND you're good at telling them.

❏ Women speakers: create your own traditions!

Chapter 3

How To Kick-Start The Planning

'People will forget what you said. They will forget what you did. But they will never forget how you made them feel.'

Maya Angelou

In the last chapter we touched on the basics, in other words the formalities of what's required of each of the main speakers. Now let's go a little deeper.

It's never too soon to begin planning your speech.

When you first start to plan your speech, it can sometimes seem a daunting task. Have no fear: you can make the planning easier by starting it early and by asking yourself some key questions.

The date and venue of the wedding are generally known well in advance. A long planning period for weddings is usual, but this can be an extra source of stress for speakers.

You, as a speaker, could be carrying that stress around with you for a year or two … unless you (a) change your mindset about stress, as I mentioned in Chapter 1, and (b) start to plan your speech at an early stage.

I'm a great believer in the power of questions. So let's approach this by the simple strategy of asking a few questions.

What are you going to say?

That is the most important question. So important that in a later chapter we're going to get into the details of how you can research, find and organise your content. Here's where we can make a start.

If you're the bride's father, you're going to begin by welcoming all the guests. But how about adding a special mention for some of the oldest, or some of those who have travelled furthest?

Then and most importantly, the central part of your speech will be all about your daughter: her life to date, her achievements and her personal qualities. Why you love her and are so proud of her. Then you'll want to talk a little about her new husband. What you like about him and why you are happy to welcome him into your family. At least I hope you are! Then you conclude your speech with a toast and you're done.

If you're the groom, your focus is, or should be, the bride. I'd go further and say that your speech could be described as representing her, unless she's also going to speak. (That's something that would have been very unusual when I got married but increasingly common nowadays.)

Maybe you'll begin by saying that this is the happiest day of your life. (If that's not how you feel, what are you doing here? I still remember just before my own wedding service, a friend crept up alongside me as I waited in the church and whispered: 'It's not too late. I've got the Alfa outside.' It was such a good line I subsequently used it myself, when a guest at the weddings of other friends.)

Many of the guests won't know how you met, so that's a very logical story and could even constitute the meat of your speech. Then you finish with a toast.

If you're the best man ... this is where we need to hear all the jokes, right?

Well, yes and no. By which I mean not necessarily, *unless* you're good at telling them.

Stories: yes. Anecdotes: yes. Reminiscences (repeatable) about experiences you and the groom have shared in the past: yes. But a best man's speech that's a collection of one-liners, many of them cut-and-pasted from the web, is the kiss of death. Your mates will enjoy them, but will everyone else?

Your opening could well be introducing yourself. The best man is often unknown to half of the wedding guests, so why not tell everyone your name, your connection to the groom, how you met, etc.

All that will get you off to a good start. And it will be great for your confidence to have had that good start. Some people say that the best man's job is the easiest. I don't agree. It depends on the personality of the person chosen. Yes, the best man is traditionally the entertainer. But you should not feel that this is compulsory. You have been chosen for this role because you are a close friend of the groom, not because you are a stand-up comedian. If you are indeed a stand-up comedian, or are in training for the profession, then that's great. But some of the finest best-man speeches

The best man as wannabe standup comic.

do not contain a single joke. Witty throwaway lines, yes. Good stories, yes. But not necessarily jokes. The perceived pressure to be funny can be an unnecessary source of extra stress for best men, in my view. Try to find stories first, and preferably stories that are personal and specific to the couple and the occasion. Those are much more likely to be remembered with affection by all the guests, not just the drunk uncles on Table 7.

And at the risk of repetition but it's a hobby-horse of mine: please, please, please don't find jokes on Google joke sites. Remember that something that you have just found, and that you think is brand new and hilarious, is travelling around the globe at the speed of light and might well have been heard already by half the audience. That's the power and the danger of the internet.

My advice, after many years of speaking at and attending

weddings, and now coaching speakers, is this: unless you are a natural joke-teller, skip the jokes. Instead, tell real-life stories which feature the bride – or more likely the groom – those are much better than jokes and they are safer. They can be either funny, or touching and romantic, so long as they are connected to the couple.

What about risqué stories, whether true or not? My advice: first run them past both the bride and groom and then judge their reaction. They'll know the guest-list in detail, whereas you might not.

If you are one of two or three or more best men, you need to work together. If more than one of the best men speaks, it is sometimes clear that they have not sat down for five minutes with their colleagues to coordinate what they are going to say. The result: lots of repetition, which is tedious and takes more time than necessary. One of my daughters says that hearing the same joke – no matter how good – told twice is the kiss of death at a wedding. Coordinating your speeches is simple; not doing so is disrespectful to the bride, the groom and the guests.

Why you?

If you are the groom, or the father of the bride, then **Why** is an unnecessary question. But if you are the best man, or best men, why were you chosen? That fact might not be obvious to all the guests so, as I mentioned above, it's worth flagging up the nature of your connection to the groom.

The value of doing this was made clear to me when I was proposing a toast recently – not at a wedding but at a special birthday party, for a very dear friend. She had guests there from all stages of her life, most of whom were strangers to me. When chatting to these strangers, the standard opening question from my side, or from theirs, was 'and what's your connection?' Those conversations reminded me of an important point: that describing your connection to the groom is the logical opening to a best man's speech.

When is everything happening?

When is already known, isn't it? It's been known for ages? Well, yes and no. Yes, the date and time of the wedding are known, so we can say for sure that your final goal is to deliver at that time a speech that is well-received by the guests in general and by the bridal party in particular, and is memorable for all the right reasons.

But if you are a planner by nature – and even if not, for this purpose I'll urge you to become one – it could make sense to break down the task into definable steps and to set target dates for each one. This will avoid the risk of your arriving at the day before the wedding still unsure what you're going to say.

Those steps could include the following. Some of them won't apply to you, but the reason for including them will become clear as you progress through this book – and which of them you need will depend partly on your personality type as well as your previous speaking experience.

The steps could be:

❑ Making a start on the planning: 'A journey of a thousand miles begins with a single step.' (Lao Tsu)

❑ Creating a mental picture of the outcome you want.

❑ Researching the audience ... that's recognised as an essential task for anyone speaking in a professional situation, but I believe it's useful for weddings too.

❑ Quizzing others for (repeatable) facts about the bride and groom … useful for best men in particular.

❑ Creating a skeleton of what you're going to say.

❑ Writing your first few paragraphs. 'The first marks on the blank sheet of paper are the hardest' (Anon.) and your closing paragraph.

❑ Completing a first draft.

❑ Completing the final text. You're probably not going to read from this on the day – unless you're very good at maintaining eye-contact while doing so – but it has its place anyway, firstly as a comfort blanket and secondly as a memento.

❑ Creating your aides-memoire. Cue cards? Mind-map? Props? We'll get to all those later.

❑ Rehearsing.

❑ More rehearsing.

Who's listening?

To be precise, who (OK, whom) are you addressing? That might seem an unnecessary question, but it's not.

The formal answer to this question depends, naturally, on your role at the wedding. If you're the father of the bride, then you're addressing the audience in general.

If you're the groom, you are mostly addressing both the guests and your bride. But in our culture you end your speech by proposing a toast to the bridesmaids in general, or to the chief bridesmaid or matron of honour or maid of honour, whichever it is on that day. So for your concluding toast you should be looking at that person or persons.

As best man, your formal role is to reply on behalf of the

last-named (and unlike the other speakers you are not by tradition required to end with a toast), so again your speech is totally addressed to the audience.

But there is more to it than that. Who are you thinking about while you are speaking? Here's the best advice I've ever heard on this subject: 'Think more about your audience, less about yourself and your performance.'

A nephew of mine – he's a musician, so he's a regular performer – told me about his experience of speaking as a best man. He said that he was very nervous in advance but a friend had boosted his confidence greatly before the event, by means of two very helpful phrases. Firstly, he said: 'it's a home crowd.' That was a great sporting analogy, reminding him that everyone there wanted the speech to succeed, which is a fact a nervous speaker could easily forget. The second thing he said was even better: 'it's not about you.'

That second statement from my nephew's friend echoes the quote in the previous paragraph. It really isn't about you; it's about your audience, so think about them and how you want them to feel, not about you and how you feel.

What do you know about the audience?

So how much do you know about them? Wedding audiences are usually quite varied. For example, knowing the age breakdown can be helpful. If you are the best man, you might have some pretty risqué stories about what you and the groom got up to in the past, and your friends might think they are fantastic. But if the bride's ninety-year-old grandmother is there too, she might not be so broad-minded (although she might be). And you as best man will not have chosen the guest list, so a little research on that matter would be good.

If there are people in the audience who have a very special connection to the occasion, it could be worth flagging that up. Most people, except the most self-effacing, like to hear their names in a speech if the connection is relevant and the context is positive. And, as I often say, that's one table that won't go to sleep during your speech.

I was speaking recently at another special birthday celebration. I happened to know that one of the other guests was a theatre director of long standing. She had discovered in my friend a previously unsuspected talent for acting and had helped her develop her talent. So I made a point of telling that story and both the hostess and her mentor friend were very happy to hear it. If you're going to be a best man, finding out that another guest has a connection with the bride that isn't widely known could work well for you. Within reason, of course.

To summarise: a little research on the audience is a worthwhile investment of time.

How are you going to do all this?

This is an essential question about presentation; but there's a strong argument for considering it last, after you're clear on your answers to the other questions.

Why last? Let me explain.

If you are someone who believes in the value of goal-setting, you might be familiar with the name of my own favourite speaker on the subject. He's a wise and witty man called Jack Black. Not the American actor of that name; this one is a Scottish trainer and author.

Black says this about setting goals: 'don't think about "how" yet, because "how" will get you every time.' He means it'll demotivate you every time, if you think about it too early in the process. First, decide what you want to achieve and by when (with those intermediate steps). Then, and only then, work out how you're going to do it.

Eventually you will be ready to decide *how* to do it. The answer lies partly in your personality, because it's important to be authentic, not to play a part. This is something that I address when I'm coaching speakers. If I were coaching you and if there's time – and there's always time, unless our first consultation is the day before the wedding – I'd ask you to complete a simple questionnaire, which would tell me some simple but all-important stuff, for example whether you are at heart an extrovert or an introvert.

Admittedly, if you are a good actor I might have got a first impression of you as an extrovert; but unless that is the real you, I shan't advise you to deliver in that style – leaving plenty of room for improvisation, for example – because it would place an unnecessary strain on you, at an occasion that's already potentially stressful. As I've suggested earlier, some very eminent actors hate public speaking, because then they have to be themselves; and actors are not necessarily extroverts, no matter what impression you might get when they are playing someone else.

Completing these kinds of personal profile (or psychometric) questionnaires typically takes just ten minutes. Remarkably, the output will then reveal a lot about the qualities that are significant in your makeup. It's your personality profile or, put another way, your preferred behavioural style. These kinds of questionnaires are widely used in recruitment … and also in marriage guidance but that's another matter. And in coaching, which is why I use them.

So, in summary, the answer to the 'how?' question is:

'it depends what kind of person you are.' Chapter 4 is all about your personality: knowing more about it, and how that information could inform your decisions about how to deliver your all-important speech.

CHECKLIST

❑ Do your research.

❑ 'A journey of a thousand miles begins with a single step.' Start planning early with these questions:

    ⭕ What am I going to say?

    ⭕ Why me? (if you're the best man)

    ⭕ What's my timeline?

    ⭕ Who's in the audience?

    ⭕ How will I do this? (i.e. best suiting my personality)

Chapter 4

What's Your Style?

'People are weird. When we find someone with weirdness that is compatible with ours, we team up and call it love.'

Dr Seuss

It goes without saying that we're all different. When it comes to speaking in public, our abilities vary. But whatever your inherent aptitude or experience as a speaker, I believe that the better you understand yourself and your personality (or your preferred behavioural style), the better you can prepare and present your speech.

When I get together with fellow writers for writerly conversations, then it won't be long before the novelists amongst us (and they tend to outnumber us boring nonfiction writers) will ask each other: 'Are you a plotter or a pantser?'

Plotters, as the name suggests, need to work out the plot in detail before they start writing. Pantsers prefer to get started with a rough structure and run with it 'by the seat of their pants.'

The equivalent questions for speakers could be 'are you

detail-oriented, with a preference for a written script? Or are you a natural raconteur, preferring to improvise from a basic structure?' You might, of course, be something in between, as life is rarely cut-and-dried.

Personal profiling questionnaires: the DISC concept

Luckily, there is a simple way to get a better understanding of your ideal style. It's in the psychometric profiling systems that are widely used in organisations these days for a totally different purpose, i.e. recruitment. There are many such tools; the one I'll suggest first, because I know more about it, is called DISC.

The way I discovered this was by coincidence. Many years ago, I was asked to design and deliver a series of training courses in presentation skills, combined with English language, for a large Norwegian chemical manufacturer. The client told me: 'our people have a good grounding in English' (that was an understatement; their knowledge in this department would shame many Brits) 'but they lack confidence in speaking the language for the purpose of business presentations. You could run these courses, because you know our business' (I'd worked in the same sector and they had recently taken over the Swedish group for which I had worked for many years) '… and you know the English language of course. So you have two of the key elements for this project. However, you don't have experience as a trainer, so we want you to work with a Norwegian management consultant whose work we like.'

That consultant and I then worked together most effectively and enjoyably over many years. Her name was Erle Bryn and we became great friends. In fact, not so long ago she came over to the UK for my 70th birthday party and then she invited me over to Oslo to be the toastmaster at her wedding.

But I digress. Apart from this lady's experience as a consultant and trainer, she was also very expert on psychometric profiling methods, of which there are many. At that time she was working particularly with the method referred to by those initials DISC, the best-known proprietary version of which was from a company called Thomas International. It's a method with which I became increasingly familiar, it's widely used in recruitment, and it's simple and quick. There are no right or wrong answers and in a recruitment scenario it reduces the risk of putting square pegs in round holes.

Knowing of my new colleague's expertise, an idea came up: 'Our trainees can't all be John F Kennedy, or Winston Churchill, or whoever you might admire as a public speaker. So why don't we use your profiling method in order to find out what raw material we're working with?'

Using psychometrics to help speakers

So we started asking the participants in our training courses to spend just ten minutes in completing a DISC questionnaire, from which a profile would be developed showing the person's scores against four personality factors. Then my colleague would give the participant a one-to-one meeting, maybe two weeks before the course, during which she would explain their own profile and what it indicated in terms of the best way for that person to present, using this new knowledge about their personality. Or, as we also called it, their preferred behavioural style.

What can this psychometric method do to improve

and facilitate your performance as a wedding speaker, particularly if speaking in public is something that you do not normally do? I believe that it can improve your planning, improve your performance and also reduce your stress level, because you know that this is using an important part of who you are. As the saying goes, 'be yourself, because everybody else is taken.' (Woody Allen, I think.)

DISC is based on the work of Dr William Marston (1893-1947), an American psychologist and inventor (also a comic book writer, who created the character Wonder Woman). I don't know how he found the time but he was also a contributor to the development of the polygraph lie detector test.

In 1928, he published *Emotions of Normal People,* which elaborated the **DISC Theory**. Marston viewed people behaving along two axes: extroverted versus introverted; and task-oriented versus people-oriented.

Where you are on each axis – and it's a spectrum: very few people are 100% one thing or the other – gives you a score against four characteristics that are unique to the DISC method. Those four characteristics are described as follows:

D for Directing (sometimes called Driving or Dominance)

I for Influencing

S for Steadiness

C for Caution (sometimes called Compliance)

Marston's theory predicts that, by comparison with the average …

- 'High D' people are more extroverted and more task-oriented.

- 'High I' people are also more extroverted … but

more people-oriented.

- 'High S' people are more introverted and more people-oriented.

- 'High C' people are more introverted and more task-oriented.

For example, if you are reading a book (this book, or any other) and if you are primarily a 'high D' style, you'll read quickly, looking for headings, shorter paragraphs and bullet points. If you are primarily a 'high I' style, you may well be interested mostly in the pictures, diagrams and headings.

And if you would worry that 'high D' and 'high I' people might be offended by the above (they won't be), then you are more likely to score highly on the S scale. If you are primarily a 'high C' style you might want more detail and the publisher's email address, in order to highlight any typos or grammatical errors that you spot. (I'm joking but only slightly.)

Here's how DISC is used in practice: you complete a multiple-choice questionnaire, as a result of which you get a profile showing your scores against those four factors.

Other psychometric profiling methods use different factors, but whichever system is used, there are no 'good' or 'bad' scores; they are all simply ways to help you understand yourself better.

For example, someone with a high 'D' factor is motivated primarily by results. Those with a high 'I' are greatly motivated by recognition (they are the people who are most likely to remember compliments they receive, as recommended by Baz Luhrmann – see Chapter 1 of this book). If you have a high 'S' you are motivated by security and want to support others; with a high 'C' you're motivated primarily by procedures and detail.

For example, I have a relatively high 'I' on the DISC chart, which means I am able to improvise when speaking in public, so I don't usually need to prepare in very great detail, so long as I have the broad themes established in advance. Yes, I could prepare everything in great detail and learn a script word-for-word, but I know that my performance will lose spontaneity.

(When speaking at a wedding, though, I modify my normal methods, because it's a big deal.)

Needless to say, but I'll say it anyway, most of us are complex animals with a mix of these characteristics. However, it's still useful to know which your strongest characteristics are.

[Some of the content of this chapter is taken from the workbook *Introduction to DISC Personality Profiling* by *The Coaching Academy* ™.]

If you'd like to know more about this and other profiling tools, a Google search under 'DISC', 'Myers Briggs', '16PF' or 'psychometric profiling' will show you links to resources, some of which are free.

'Be authentic!' What does that mean? Joanna Penn's insights

Lots of public speaking experts say 'be authentic' but what exactly does that mean?

I'm towards the extrovert end of the spectrum. But I remembered from courses that I used to run that other personality types had special strengths for the purpose of speaking but they would not be so obvious to me. So I decided to consult others who know about this. For example, there are benefits to a speaker in being an introvert; in fact, many writers, coaches and bloggers actually claim that introverts make the best speakers.

The best book I've come across on the topic is by Joanna Penn and it's called *Public Speaking for Authors, Creatives and Other Introverts* (See Resources for a link). I can attest personally to the fact that Ms Penn is a very accomplished (and frequent) public speaker; in fact she's in constant demand to speak at, for example, conferences about self-publishing, a subject on which she's an acknowledged expert. Yet despite her assured performances at scores of events, she is by her own admission an introvert. So if anyone knows about this, it's Ms Penn. By kind permission I quote here some of the things she says in her book.

P.S. As I said, I am towards the extrovert end of the spectrum. But Joanna Penn's book reminded me that it's not an either / or situation and that some of my behaviours echo hers.

Extracts from *PUBLIC SPEAKING FOR AUTHORS, CREATIVES AND OTHER INTROVERTS* by Joanna Penn

(https://amzn.to/2JFbh4K)

- We're all different, and we all exist on the spectrum of personality. There are no absolutes, and we move up and down the scale, even during the span of a single day. There is no 'better' type of personality, and no value judgment as to where you sit.

- What is an introvert? 'Introverts are drawn to the inner world of thought and feeling, extroverts to the external life of people and activities. Introverts focus on the meaning they make of the events swirling around them; extroverts plunge into the events themselves. Introverts recharge their batteries by being alone; extroverts need to recharge when they don't socialize enough.' Susan Cain, *Quiet: The Power of Introverts in a World That Won't Stop Talking.*

- 'Introverts think carefully before they speak. We can be excellent public speakers because we prepare carefully.' Sophia Dembling, *The Introvert's Way: Living a Quiet Life in a Noisy World.*

- When I first started my journey of public speaking, I thought that I had to develop another, separate, persona for the 'stage.' I had spent years in the corporate environment developing an extroverted shell because I thought that the real 'me' wasn't acceptable. I thought I needed to do the same thing as a speaker.

- I'm happy sharing my intimate thoughts and ideas through writing and online, and prefer to communicate using the written word.

- If you recognize yourself in any of these points, I highly recommend that you read *Quiet* by Susan Cain, or watch her TED talk on the power of introverts.

- One popular way to see where you sit on the spectrum is to take a Myers Briggs test. There are free options online. Of course, it's a blunt tool but it may be interesting to see your results. I am INFJ, a common personality type amongst writers.

- Preparation is one of the most important things, especially as a new speaker, regardless of personality type. Structure helps with your confidence.

- When you craft a talk, you have to organize your thoughts into a coherent structure and lead people through a story. This helps to order your own thoughts, and can change the way in which you think about a topic.

- Being comfortable with your body and being seen is critical in a speaker. I did a training course nearly ten years ago now and one of the exercises involved just standing up in front of the group and being looked at for several minutes, without speaking. The feeling of being watched is something that you need to get used to, and the only way to do that is to experience it. As the speaker, there's a moment when the eyes of the people in the room fall on you, and you can get the attention of an audience just by standing silently, no need to hush them. Your presence can be powerful. Just practise standing tall and being aware of your body.

- Carry painkillers for a possible headache.

- You can make people laugh with life situations and stories, but not by Googling the joke of the day. Laughing at yourself, being humble and authentic goes a long way with any audience.

- Speaking is about the audience, but it's also about you. When you're 'on' you need to become a 150% version of you, but the energy that you bring to the speaking platform isn't something that can be lived in all the time. We all portray different sides of ourselves in a variety of situations. We behave differently with our partners than when we are with our parents, children or work colleagues. That's just different sides of you, and they are all genuine and real. So, your speaking is kind of a performance, but it should also be an authentic one.

[Reproduced by kind permission of the author.

Find Joanna's books, blog and podcast at
www.TheCreativePenn.com]

Personality traits: a neuroscientist's view

I recently heard a fascinating radio programme fronted by the excellent historian Bettany Hughes. It was part of a BBC Radio 4 series called *The Ideas That Make Us* and this episode was called Character. She began with the original Greek meaning of the word: an impression or imprint. That of course leads to one of the modern meanings of the word, i.e. a symbol representing a letter or number.

Then she proceeded to the modern (from the time of the Scottish Enlightenment, if I remember correctly, so the word 'modern' is relative) meaning of characteristics of an individual. One of her guests, Professor Patrick Haggard from the Institute of Cognitive Neuroscience at University

College London, listed what he called 'the big five factors', or personality traits:

- extraversion

- openness

- agreeableness

- conscientiousness

- neuroticism

Prof Haggard went on to say that if you can define how a person measures against these factors, you have captured their character ... and you can guess how long they are likely to live, how happy they will be, and many other features of their life.

Interesting stuff. I'm not sure where it takes us in connection with public speaking but I hope that by the time I publish the second edition of this book I will come up with something.

CHECKLIST

- ❑ What does this chapter tell you about your ideal method of preparing a speech?

- ❑ What does it tell you about how to deliver a speech?

Chapter 5

The Words

'If you want me to speak for twenty minutes, I need two weeks' warning. But if you want me to speak for two hours, I can begin now.'

Winston Churchill

This chapter is about content. This is where we expand the 'what are you going to say?' in Chapter 3. For me, that's partly a question of my thought process and partly a matter of how I record the output of that process. As somebody once said, 'how do I know what I think until I see what I've written?' So I'll begin by talking about how I write down my thoughts and make a first draft.

'The Foolscap Manifesto'

The foolscap manifesto is a phrase that I picked up from a book called *Do the Work* by Stephen Pressfield. It is a concept I like and I now use when I'm starting out with a new project or idea. According to Pressfield almost any project, even the plot of a three-act play or a novel or a movie screenplay, can be summarised on a single sheet of foolscap paper. Let's be international and call it A4 paper, which is almost the same size.

So if it's good for a three-act play, it's good for the outline of a speech: (1) beginning, (2) middle, (3) end. I've used that system for the first draft of speeches, most recently for my daughter's wedding. For example: (1) Welcomes, (2) Stories, (3) Conclusion/toast.

Is this an idea that you can use to draft your speech? They do say that the first marks on a sheet of paper are the hardest and they also say that in a journey of 1000 miles the first step is the most important. OK, enough clichés. To details:

My version of the foolscap manifesto is always done on a legal pad, as our American friends call it; and for me it has to be yellow. Somebody who was sitting at the next table in a cafe once told me why yellow paper is best. She was studying neuroscience at university and she explained there was a logical reason for this. Why did I get into conversation with her? Because I noticed that she too was using a coloured legal pad. Admittedly hers was pink: I haven't gone that far yet. As far as I understood her explanation, I think it was about the words embedding themselves more quickly if they are written on coloured stock. Some people however say that the benefit is more mundane, i.e. in a file containing both handwritten notes and typescripts, the handwritten notes are immediately distinguishable if on coloured stock.

All I can tell you is that it works for me. Therefore when I saw a TV documentary about the supergroup The Traveling Wilburys I was delighted to see Bob Dylan in a sound booth laying down a vocal track, singing lyrics which had been handwritten minutes before on a yellow legal pad.

The power of stories

I am a great believer in the power of stories. In fact a fellow-coach and I launched a series of workshops based on this power, a couple of years ago. If you met my daughters, they would probably tell you that the best holidays of their childhood were when we went to something called Campus. I say 'something' advisedly, because it was unique or at least very hard to define. I have described it to friends as a cross between a camping holiday in Devon and an arts festival and because I don't much like camping it must be that they got the balance exactly right.

But I think there's a special reason my girls loved it so much. All the families – and it was only families, with singletons and child-free couples politely turned away – pitched their tents in squares which were called villages. Each village had a small marquee in the corner, occupied by a couple employed as 'village parents'. They would provide a continental breakfast (if you wanted a cooked one, you headed over to the main catering area where cooked food, mostly of the healthy variety, was available), and newspapers in the mornings. However, their starring role happened in the evenings. Weather permitting, those village parents would light a fire and we would all check our kids in with them and head off to the central marquees for drinks, dinner and entertainment. Meanwhile our children, tucked up in their sleeping bags, would be ranged around the fire, where they would toast marshmallows. Then, best of all, professional storytellers would arrive, enchanting the kids as dusk fell. My daughters remember this with great fondness and therefore, ever since, I have had high respect for storytellers.

Those particular storytellers were mostly actors in between jobs. Nowadays, when I meet someone who describes herself as a professional storyteller, I'm going to listen when they tell me their opinions on wedding speeches. The one I met recently was called Polly Tisdall and you'll find her views in the 'Tips from the Pros' section.

The point of my story is that stories are powerful. That experience in the fields of Devon has stayed for twenty years in the memories of my children and the many hundreds of children who attended those holidays. And as Maya Angelou said, '… people will never forget how you made them feel.' So tell stories.

The speeches

The Father of the Bride

The Father of the Bride's speech is always the first, according to our traditions.

In the past, the bride's family was responsible for the entire cost of the wedding. Nowadays the couple themselves often pay part or all of the wedding costs. That doesn't change the fact that the father of the bride usually speaks first.

By 'father of the bride' I mean whoever has taken on that role at the wedding. So I include under this heading not only the bride's father but maybe her stepfather, maybe a brother. It's whoever 'gives her away', to use our quaint and somewhat anachronistic term. For second marriages, the role is sometimes taken by a son. I once fulfilled this role for a neighbour's family. Although I wasn't a relative,

I was 'giving the bride away', so I gave that first speech.

This first speech is generally given at the end of the meal (or 'wedding breakfast', as we used to call it). In fact the British tradition has been that for any formal occasion that involves a meal and speeches, those speeches are all at the end of the meal. By contrast, at dinner parties in some other cultures (for example in Sweden), a host might make a short speech of welcome in which every guest is welcomed with some appropriate words addressed to each one in turn; and that speech is at the start of the meal. Then the speaker can relax and enjoy the meal and the drinks.

I was giving a Father of the Bride speech recently and I was very glad that my daughter decided to follow the lead of those sensible Swedes.

She's not the only one: at British weddings more and more couples are deciding to spread the speeches out throughout the meal. I welcome the trend.

So ... what are you going to say?

Your primary tasks are threefold: to welcome the guests (in this context you speak as if you are the host, whether or not you are paying the costs of the wedding); then to tell everyone what a wonderful person the bride is (in case they didn't know) and to say something about the groom; and finally to propose a toast. Your toast will be 'the bride and groom'.

So your first job is to welcome the guests. Even though you won't know them all personally, and even though the event has perhaps been going for a couple of hours when you start speaking, this task is paramount.

A simple phrase of welcome is enough; but it's always nice to add something. For example, you could make a special mention of anybody who has come a particularly long way; and / or some of the very oldest guests; and any guests that the bride and groom think should have a special mention. This last point illustrates the crucial importance of speakers coordinating in advance with each other.

Then, and most importantly, the central part of your speech will be all about your daughter: her life to date, her achievements and her personal qualities. Why you love her and are so proud of her.

Those are the basics; but how can you improve on that? You will, of course, have lots of things to say based on your experience of your daughter; stories about her life so far – and this is where it's fine to include amusing stories, given that you as her dad won't repeat any embarrassing stories – and what you perceive as her best qualities. But maybe you can improve on that by asking your extended family. The bride's mother, if she's not speaking herself, will probably have stories that she remembers and you don't; I certainly found that to be the case. And what about uncles, aunts, cousins, family friends?

Then you'll want to talk a little about her new husband. What you like about him and why you are happy to welcome him into your family. At least I hope you are. Then you conclude your speech with a toast and you're done. Your toast will be 'to X and Y, the bride and groom.'

The Groom

The Groom's Speech usually follows the Father of the Bride's Speech.

You're responding on behalf of both of you, thanking those who've helped with the day, finishing by proposing a toast.

Firstly you'll reply, on behalf of your bride and yourself,

to the toast just proposed by the bride's father. And you'll thank him for the very positive things he has – hopefully – just said about you. I remember that on my own wedding day, my new father-in-law most certainly did that, so I said I hoped I could live up to his compliments and expectations.

You might want to add and personalise some words of welcome to the guests, in addition to those already said by your bride's father. After all, you probably know them all, which he might not. Unless you have had a chance to consult with him in advance, this is something you'll have to improvise.

You'll probably want to thank those who have helped to organise the day, and those who have paid for it, if it wasn't you and your bride.

Naturally and most importantly, you will want to say something good about your new wife. Actually, something very good indeed about your wife: that would be my advice.

The traditional conclusion to the groom's speech is a toast to the bridesmaids in general, or to the chief bridesmaid, or maid of honour; or matron of honour if she herself is married. Whatever she's called at your wedding, the bride's chief attendant is the person that the groom concludes by toasting. This tradition is starting to die out, however, and so you might like to consider other options, such as all the parents and grandparents present.

The Best Man

The formal demand on the best man at a British wedding is simple: to respond to the groom's final toast. If tradition has been followed, then you're responding on behalf of the bridesmaids in general, or the chief bridesmaid (or maid of honour) in particular.

You do not have to conclude with a toast, although many best men repeat the toast to the bride and groom. What matters most is how you personalise your speech and how you put it across with feeling.

When deciding what to say, the first question to ask and answer is: why you? That's something that many guests won't know; so tell that story. Do tell stories about the couple, your part in their story so far, your previous life as the groom's friend, etc. Please don't scour the web for jokes: that's a strategy that has killed many wedding receptions. If you're a natural joke-teller, then great, but do personalise them. Stories are great; recycled jokes are not.

A final tip for best men: reading out messages, from distant relatives or friends who couldn't make it, is a wonderful excuse for writing out and reading some imaginary messages. Back in the day, they were telegrams, but the opportunity for invention has survived the end of the telegram era. And knowing that part of your speech involves reading out from a piece of paper is a great way to settle the nerves.

The Best Man as Toastmaster

Many couples nowadays hire a Toastmaster (or Master of Ceremonies) if their budget allows. According to the Guild of International Professional Toastmasters:

Toastmaster is a general term, referring to a person in charge of the proceedings ...

... typically charged with organisation of the event, arranging the order of speakers, introducing one or more of the speakers, and keeping the event on schedule.

... the toastmaster often takes the form of a master of

ceremonies, introducing the entertainment acts.

Keeping things on schedule, introducing the speakers, maybe introducing the band later, are all worthwhile things to outsource. Moreover the toastmaster's scarlet costume adds a great splash of colour.

If the budget doesn't allow, the best man is sometimes asked to perform the duties of toastmaster. In this case, the duties are usually limited to introducing the speeches. But any best man who is at the extraversion end of the spectrum (see Chapter 4) will probably relish this extra duty, in my experience.

All you have to do is:

- In advance, find out from the couple when they want the speeches to start.

- At the appropriate time, get everyone's attention. The traditional way of doing that is by tapping a spoon several times on the rim of a glass (preferably without breaking the glass). With the help of PA it's amazing how effective this can be.

- Using the microphone if available, make this announcement:

- 'Ladies and Gentlemen, play silence for Mr xxxx yyyy, the Father of the Bride, who will propose a toast to the Bride and Groom.'

OR …

- 'Ladies and Gentlemen, pray silence for Mr xxxx yyyy, who will propose the Father of the Bride's toast.'

(NOTE: this latter wording covers the fact that although in our culture this first speech always concludes with a toast, it is sometimes delivered by someone other than the bride's father. For example a stepfather, a brother, etc.)

Now you lead the applause for that first speech. And simply leading applause for anything is a great stress-reliever for a speaker.

If the bride is going to speak (an increasingly common occurrence nowadays and a welcome one) then this is the logical place for her to do it, so you'll say:

'Ladies and Gentlemen, play silence for Mrs xxxx yyyy, the Bride.'

Lead the applause, then:

'Ladies and Gentlemen, pray silence for Mr xxxx yyyy, the Bridegroom.'

Now you'll simply lead the applause for the groom's speech – and any other speeches if there are any - and then go straight into your own speech.

Other speakers … the bride, the bride's mother, the maid of honour …

Although our traditions in the past provided for just three speeches (all by men), more and more brides are now choosing to speak at their own weddings. Not before time.

In other countries it has been different for some time. I once spoke at a fiftieth birthday party in Sweden (where that particular birthday is a very big deal) and more recently I've been the toastmaster at a large wedding reception in Norway. At both of these events, there were lots of speakers (about a dozen each time) and half of them were women.

Here's the good news for any female speaker at a wedding, or for any speaker apart from the three main ones … there are no traditions about what you should or should not say. It's simply a matter for your good taste and your good sense. All I'll say is: invest enough time to plan what you're going to say; and whether you'll be using PA or not, make sure you can be heard by everyone in the room.

CHECKLIST

- ❏ Review the section above that refers to your part of the proceedings
- ❏ Do you already have the resources, stories etc. that you need? If not, where will you find them?
- ❏ Talk to the other speakers in advance. Even though a wedding audience is always polite, they won't want to hear the same things twice. Coordination is key!
- ❏ When you've made your first draft, read it aloud and time it. Aim for between five and ten minutes.

Chapter 6

How To Remember It All

'Memory is a fickle friend. It something something in the end.'

Ian Martin

So you've done the thinking and the research and you have a first draft, then a second, and finally a finished speech with which you are happy. How can you make sure you remember it on the day?

In 'the good old days', the standard method of remembering a speech was simple. You planned your speech, you wrote it out (or typed it out) and you read from it. That way you could be sure to remember everything.

Reading from a typescript, however, has disadvantages. Firstly, it is difficult to keep eye contact with the audience – and eye contact is an important part of keeping an audience engaged. Secondly, it is difficult to read from a script and sound convincing, to be animated, or in fact to show any emotion.

On this very special day, that's not what we want. As the saying goes (I'm quoting Maya Angelou): '… people will forget what you said. They will forget what you did. But they will never forget how you made them feel.' If you read your speech, even if your choice of words is perfect and you read it beautifully, the chances are that they will feel very little if your eyes are on the paper all the time.

Disappointing speeches

One of the most disappointing speeches I have ever heard should have been one of the most interesting. It was genuinely public speaking, in other words it was at a large meeting, about public services in the city where I was living at the time, and the speakers were all top people in the city.

One particular speaker was in charge of an area of policy in which I was extremely interested, so I had looked forward to his speech greatly. To my disappointment, he read from a script from start to finish; and he rarely lifted his eyes from the paper. Later, during the question and answer session, one of his answers made me wonder how this man ever got his job; but I had already formed that impression because of the way he had delivered his speech.

Reading that speech from start to finish also made me wonder if he had even written it himself. As he was a director employed by the council, he no doubt had a staff and he probably delegated the speechwriting to a member of that staff. The fact he hadn't prepared sufficiently, whatever the reasons, gave a poor impression.

Do you want to give that impression when you are speaking at a wedding? The impression that somebody else wrote your speech and you didn't have time to learn it?

Reading from the page

I have explained my concern about people reading from a

script but there are other considerations that might make it necessary or, at least, desirable.

For years I preferred improvising around main points on cue cards, because I'm towards the extrovert end of the spectrum (see Chapter 4 about the effect of personality). However, I changed my mind when I spoke at my daughter's wedding last year for reasons I shall explain. I recognise too that many people feel they couldn't face giving the speech without reading it, or at least the important parts of it. And a wedding speech can cause more than usual amounts of stress, even for experienced speakers.

Why does it cause extra stress? Because it matters. Recently, I watched the usually-unflappable and always-on-TV Stephen Fry, speaking in a televised debate. He began his speech with these words: 'I've been really nervous all day. Why? Because this subject / debate / motion matters to me.'

For anyone who has seen Fry on television hosting the quiz show *QI*, or hosting the BAFTA (British Academy of Film and Television Arts) film awards twelve times, it's hard to believe he could ever be really nervous. What Fry said on that occasion illustrates an important point: the more something matters to you, the more nervous you are likely to be.

So I too was extremely nervous when preparing to speak at my daughter's wedding. Because it mattered. However, my change of heart about having a typescript to hand, either to read from or as a backup, had begun with a random conversation a year or two ago. My estimable writing coach Jacqui Lofthouse told me that when she got married, her husband (talented cartoonist David Lewis, who provided the illustrations for this book) gave a wonderful speech, which he read throughout. The key, she said, was that he knew where to pause and make eye contact with the audience. In that way it didn't feel as if it was being read. And of course the benefit was that he would have been sure that he didn't miss a single word of a speech that he'd taken a lot of time to prepare. Hearing that story reminded me that it can be done, so maybe I should revise my former prejudices.

Even so, when my daughter's wedding came around and I was planning my speech in the preceding months, I still had no intention of reading from a script, or even having my written script with me. I'd planned to use cue-cards, as I'd done for years.

My last-minute adjustment

I changed my mind a few days beforehand. Why? My rationale was this: I'd put a lot of thought into the content: not just the structure and the stories but the actual words. This would be a short speech of about ten minutes, which I was confident I could learn by heart. I knew I might well throw in some ad-libs, but I wanted to be sure I didn't miss anything that I'd planned to say.

If I lost my way, I wanted to have the exact words to refer to. I didn't want to have bullet points on a cue-card around which I'd extemporise; that would be fine for most situations but not for my daughter's wedding. So I learned the text and took the typescript with me.

Other circumstances under which it's absolutely fine to read

Firstly, and obviously, it's fine to read from your typescript if you can't find another way of remembering the content of the speech. If you do that, it's important to pause between paragraphs in order to lift your eyes from the page and reconnect with the listeners.

Secondly, if the nerves of the occasion have become so severe that another solution cannot be found.

Thirdly, if there are parts of the speech where you are repeating somebody else's words, it's absolutely fine to read from a piece of paper in order to be sure of getting those words 100% right. An obvious example is that in the past the best man's duties included reading the telegrams that had been received. Naturally it was OK to read those telegrams; it wasn't necessary to memorise them. Today, when there are no telegrams, we extend that sometimes to reading the messages, for example that card sent by Aunt Mollie in Australia who couldn't attend the wedding.

Fourthly, you might decide to use a piece of poetry or prose to illuminate the speech and it's absolutely fine to read that from a typescript. I've noticed that there are businesses now that will even provide you with a piece of poetry or prose that's personalised to your wedding. You'd read that out, for sure. And in fact if you use any text written by someone else to illuminate your speech it's absolutely fine to read that from a typescript. Why? Because they are someone else's words and you owe it that person to get them 100% right.

Maybe you are familiar with the term 'belt and braces' and here's a good example. Even if you decide to go with another type of aide-memoire (see below), it's absolutely fine to have a typescript of the whole speech and to take it with you as a 'comfort blanket'. Some best men, for example, give a copy of their speech to the couple as a memento and that's a nice gesture. Even better if framed!

The best way to read from a script

If you're going to read from your typescript for whatever reason, there's a simple way to make your performance as compelling as it can be. Carefully go through your speech and mark, for example with a highlighter pen, the key passages: the ones you want to emphasise. Then, after each highlighted passage, pause ... lift your eyes from the page ... make eye contact with the audience ... then go back to the page.

Even if those pauses seem very long to you, they will not be too long in reality; that's a well-known by-product of adrenaline. If you don't believe me, try out this technique in advance with a friend or partner.

Alternatives to reading from a script

So what are the alternatives to reading from a script, or having it there as a backup in case you get lost? They divide into three main categories: cue cards (sometimes called prompt cards), mind maps and props.

Cue cards

These are small (say 3 by 5 inches) cards: small enough to hold in your hand but large enough to write a few words on each: the 'bullet points' of your speech. They are a great aide-memoire, **provided** you don't write too much on each card: just a few lines of writing or typescript; and just a few words on each line. If you've rehearsed your speech enough (which you must; and which I will come on to), then just a few words will remind you of the next topic.

Mind-maps

These are great if you know how to use them, and they are a technique that I find very useful. If you're familiar with them, then you know the advantages and you know how to prepare them, whether hand-drawn or using mind-mapping software, of which there are many versions available as free downloads.

However, if you don't yet have the knowhow, then I am reminded of the words of bandleader and composer Duke Ellington, when asked the meaning of the word 'swing.' He said: 'if you gotta ask, don't mess with it.' That's my way of saying that if you are not already familiar with mind-mapping then I suggest you avoid it for this important task. A wedding speech is not the place to experiment with a new technique.

Many years ago, I 'stood in' as father of the bride for a neighbour's daughter. On that occasion I decided to use a mind-map. And I had that speech with me exactly as that mind-map. One of my daughters looked at the mind-map and asked 'what's that, Daddy?'

'That's a mind-map,' I said, rather grandly, assuming she wouldn't be familiar with the concept. 'It helps me to picture and remember my speech.' The reply from this grown-up twelve-year-old: 'Oh yes, I remember those. We learned them at primary school. We called them spidergrams.' Primary school, eh? Not the first or the last time that this father would be shown up (always unintentionally, I hasten to add) by his daughters.

Props

Props are my favourite aide-memoire if you're making a

Best Man speech. The first and best example of this method I have ever seen was at a wedding in Norway. The best man had a large bag, from which he produced a series of artefacts, many of which he had made himself. Each one represented a story from the past: in other words, they were experiences he had shared with the groom. It was a win / win: for him, because he didn't need any written notes and each artefact prompted a story; for the audience, because of the anticipation and the drama: 'what's coming out of the bag next?'

He had added practicality to creativity: each artefact was joined to the next one by a length of ribbon, so that they would necessarily come out of the bag in chronological order. (That's a 'nice-to-have' feature, if you'd like to try this method.)

More on cue-cards

Despite what I said about changing my method and forgoing cue-cards for my daughter's wedding, I have been using cue-cards for many years for all kinds of speeches, so I felt I should write more about them. But then I learned about an excellent site full of speaking resources. It's called write-out-loud. It's the kind of site I wish I had written. And it has a very useful page on cue cards, which I reproduce here by kind permission of the site's owner.

Cue cards: how to make and use them effectively

Making cue cards from standard office supply index or note cards is relatively easy. Using them well will lift the quality of your presentation immeasurably.
Why?
The answer is simple.

Because you are not relying on, and reading from, a word-for-word text you are free to interact with your audience.

You are able to:

make eye contact,

respond,

gesture

and move freely.

You will sound, look and feel more present; 'in the moment'. Your entire delivery is enlivened.

For those of you who are nervous about making the transition from a full script to note cards, don't be. Take it slowly. Give yourself time to thoroughly rehearse. You'll be delighted with the result.

How to make cue cards

You need a packet of standard index cards, a selection of highlighters, (for example, yellow, pink, blue and green), and an easily-read pen. I suggest using one with either blue or black ink.

The best (most useful) cue cards (https://www.write-out-loud.com/cue-cards.html#The-Best-Cue-Cards):

1. *have ONE main heading or idea per card*
2. *are written clearly using larger than usual font (so you can read them easily)*
3. *have plenty of white space around each word or phrase to help them stand out*
4. *use bullet points or numbers to itemize the supporting ideas under the main heading*
5. *are written on ONE side of the card only*
6. *are clearly numbered so that you know the order they come in and/or they may even be tied together. (Drill a hole through the left corner and tie with a*

loop of string so that the cards can be flipped.)

7. are **color-coded** to show your main idea, supporting ideas, examples and transitions or links.

8. **have where props are to be shown**. For example: Main Idea One - Supporting Idea - Example - Show slide 1

9. **have approximate timings marked** so you can track yourself through your allotted time. If you find you're going over you can adjust by leaving out an extra example or conversely if you're under time, you can add one in.

Preparing your speech for cue cards
Before starting on the cue cards themselves make sure you've got the flow of the speech how you want it. Using your speech outline go through from the beginning checking the sequence of ideas, supporting material and their transitions to ensure all your information is in an effective and logical sequence. Do try it out loud and time it. You may need to edit if it's too long and it's a lot easier to do that at this stage. Once you have the length right for your time allowance, if possible get other people to listen to you. Have them give you feedback on content, structure and delivery; paying particular attention to the introduction and the close. When you're satisfied you have your speech as you want it, you're ready to prepare it for cue cards.

Writing up your cue cards
Each segment of your speech, from its introduction to conclusion, should be reducible to a key word or phrase that will act as a prompt triggering your memory for what it was you wanted to say.

Go through your outline marking each of them. A good way to identify them is to remember the paragraphing structure that you use in written prose. A new thought or idea takes a new paragraph. In writing note cards a new idea or thought equals a new card.

Do not be tempted to write the whole of the text of your speech out. This defeats your purpose. You'll finish with cramped notes that, as well as being difficult to read, stop you from freely interacting with your audience.

Once you've finished identifying segments and giving each a keyword or phrase you're ready to write up your cards using the 1-9 guidelines above.

Decide on the color coding you're going to use e.g. pink for main ideas and blue for supporting ones. Yellow is for quotes and important facts. Green is for transitions.

Number each card as you go in the same place. The top right hand corner works well for me. I also write which part of the speech the card is for: introduction, body and conclusion as a heading in the top left. It helps me keep track of where I'm up to.

Double check the effectiveness of each card as you write them to make sure you are using keywords or phrases that actually do trigger your memory. This is particularly important for links or transitions. Forgetting how you got from one piece of information to the next not only leaves you stranded but your audience as well.

Reproduced by kind permission of Susan Dugdale, www.write-out-loud.com

'Learning your lines'

How practical is it to learn your speech by heart, so that you only need your typescript there as a backup, a comfort blanket? Actors have to remember great chunks of script, page after page, but luckily you don't have to do that. You'd 'only' need to remember five to ten minutes of material. So I asked my daughter Madeleine, who is a professional actor, for her Top Tips about learning scripts.

I'm about to teach you a really easy and quick way to memorise words that requires no effort at all.

I'm lying. Of course I'm not about to do that. We'd all love that to be possible, but until we're all half robot and can upload information like data, the only way is practice. There really is no shortcut. I know, it's disappointing, but true.

HOWEVER, there are some ways of making it easier. Different brains work different ways. Some people have a very visual memory, others kinaesthetic (to do with how you move). Ever woken up at home after a heavy night and wondered how you got there? Your body got you there because it remembers the way home.

If you've ever revised for an exam you'll remember that some bits of information stuck better than others.

Visual learners *often respond well to pictures or words in different colours to trigger memories. Ever struggled to remember someone's name but been certain of what that person wore the last time you saw them or associate a colour strongly with them? You can remember the album cover image of an old favourite, but not the name. You probably have quite a visual memory.*

Kinaesthetic learners *will plot out actions with*

their bodies. Dancers either naturally have, or soon develop, very good kinaesthetic memory. They get to the stage where their body knows a routine better than their brain does. I bet plenty of 90s kids still remember 'the macarena' or Whigfield's school disco classic 'Saturday Night' - your brain has stored that somewhere so your body remembers it without you having to (we won't judge you). If you're someone who finds these things really easy, you might lean towards a kinaesthetic memory.

I believe most people are a mix of the two, but identifying which you lean towards will help you put information into it.

*For **visual learners**, I would recommend taking your speech and truncating it down to cue cards with keywords, supported by images and different colours. Put a picture on it of the event you want to talk about if you fancy (careful not to leave it lying on the table during the disco afterwards if it includes incriminating content!). Whatever will help you get into the mindframe of that anecdote or memory. You know your story better than anyone else, and sometimes a natural re-wording in the moment makes for a very authentic speech.*

*For **kinaesthetic learners**, I would recommend doing something physical while you practise. Get up and walk around. If you like walking or running, run your speech on a jog. You'll probably find yourself connecting little movements to words. There is a speed-line learning technique I learned from a director that he called 'English for foreigners'. You have to act out the whole speech word by word as if the person you're* *talking to doesn't understand the word you're using. Effectively, you 'act out' every single word (while saying it) in a very over the top way, and your body learns it as if it's a dance routine. Granted, you might feel like a complete plonker doing it at home on your own, but it really really works.*

Even as a mostly visual learner, I've used that exercise lots and it's the closest thing to a magic wand that I've found.

It can be done. And it can be done in a handful of days if needed. Remember to give yourself breaks, just like revising for an exam; your brain - just like your computer - will usually needs a 'restart' after an update. Have a break, have a sleep and try again tomorrow, you'll be amazed at how much has gone in.

To Madeleine's advice I'd add this: for an auditory learner, which I am (primarily), the way that works for me is to record my speech and play it over and over again. For a professional actor, that probably wouldn't work, but when you need to learn a ten-minute speech, it can work very effectively. And most mobile phones nowadays have a voice recorder app. Mine has, although it's a five-year-old model.

As to how many times you should listen to your recording of the speech, that's your decision. All I will say is: 'the more times the better'.

CHECKLIST

- ❏ Decide which kind of aide-memoire suits you best
- ❏ Prepare your resources (aides-memoire) only when you've finalised the speech
- ❏ Even if you don't plan to read from a typescript, print a copy as a comfort blanket. And print a second copy as backup!
- ❏ If you're going to read out material written by others (e.g. messages, poetry, prose), have typed copies of those ready.

Chapter 7

Finding Your Voice

'Once in a lifetime, a voice like Frank Sinatra's comes along. Why did it have to be in mine?'
Bing Crosby

You'll probably have heard the old saying that a chain is only as strong as its weakest link. With that in mind, what a pity it would be if you've crafted a wonderful speech but people can't hear you. So this chapter is about making sure that your voice can carry your words to every single member of the audience. The challenges are different depending on whether or not you'll be using a PA system, so I'll deal with those challenges separately.

Cicely Berry, the eminent former Voice Director of the Royal Shakespeare Company from 1969 to 2014, wrote a book called *Your Voice and How to Use It: the classic guide to speaking with confidence.* It's a sort of bible on the subject. It is aimed at speakers of all kinds but wedding speeches are evidently in focus, as one of the three photos on the cover is of a wedding top table. If you really want to go for broke, I recommend that book, as the many exercises contained in it have the imprimatur of the world-famous RSC.

Most wedding speakers don't need to go to that degree of study, especially as PA systems are so widely used nowadays and anyway Shakespearean actors need to develop greater powers of projection than you will ever need.

However, some simple vocal warmups are always a good idea, so you'll find some in this chapter if you don't want to study the detail of Cicely Berry's book.

With PA (Public Address System)

The use of PA is now widespread at weddings, so let's start with that. One of the 'worst crimes' of any speaker is not being heard. And that means by everyone in the room, even old Uncle Fred in the back row. Unless the venue is really small, if a PA is available then I really urge you to use it.

If you've never used a microphone before, or if you are resistant to the idea for any reason, then talk to any of your friends who are musicians or who have used PA for any reason. Get their advice and try out a mic in advance. It's well worth the trouble.

Meanwhile, here's some advice gleaned from my own experience and that of my friends and relations.

For many years during my own speaking career, I've always believed you should use a lapel mic if it's available. That way your hands are free and you can move about if you want to.

However, at a wedding everything is different, in this as in so many respects. Because there are multiple speakers and all the speeches are generally short, fitting a lapel mic to each speaker in turn and then switching it just a few minutes later would be an unnecessary complication, unless the wedding has a monster sound setup.

There might be a stand for the mic and that's OK, provided you keep your head still so that you stay close to the mic.

Some singers say 'eat the mic' (not literally; but keep it close). On the occasions I've used a hand-held in the past I always followed this advice and held the mic close to my mouth. For my own daughter's wedding, I changed my method, because of something she'd said. Caroline is a surgical registrar in a hospital and as part of her training she'd worked a year teaching medical students and recently qualified doctors. For that role she was given professional tuition for her teaching, which was usually PA-aided. She was taught not to hold the mic up close but down in front of one's chest.

So I tried that and it worked; at least for that type of mic. It depends how directional the mic is. The bonus: the mic was out of my eye-line and it was easier to brace the hand holding it. Another case of 'it's what you learn after you know it all that counts.'

Microphone technique

My younger daughter Madeleine is a professional actor and singer. She has lots of experience using microphones of all kinds when doing cabaret, musical theatre and panto. Here's her advice:

What is it?
Handheld microphones are all pretty similar to use, with small differences.
Lead vs. cordless (good old technology). It shouldn't affect you unless you're planning on going on a wander to talk to the crowd (see my brother-in-law's epic groom speech for examples!). With a lead, you're

more restricted, obviously, but if you're graced with cordless and decide to go wandering, check where the speakers are. If you've ever been to a gig, you'll have heard of 'feedback'. It happens when a microphone gets too close to a speaker, and isn't nice for anyone, so if it happens just move away from the speaker.

Is there an on/off switch? SO basic, but have a look. With everything else to think about, it's easier to get caught out than you think. And if the person who spoke before you was nervous, they might turn it off in relief as they hand it over.

What do I do with it?

Ideally you want to hold it just under your mouth so it feels like you're speaking over the top of it. Have a look at stand-up comedians, they're not snogging it like Liam Gallagher or holding it a metre from their mouth like Celine Dion. And unless you're planning on breaking into a power ballad, under the mouth is best. You'll soon work out if people can hear you. If you're not sure, ask them. If not, they'll soon tell you. Nothing like a wave of 'we can't hear you' rippling through the crowd to make you feel like you're back in school assembly.

(I went to a quiz recently where two people alternated using the same mic and over the course of an hour one of them didn't work out that she held it at her side for the whole thing, despite the crowd having to ask for EVERY single question again. Eggy.)

Listen to the room and when you practise your speech, practise holding something too. That's right folks, it's hairbrush microphone time. Trust me, it's worth it.

What's HaPPening?

Some 'plosive' sounds (B's and P's) shoot out a higher concentration of air out as you say them, and when speaking into a mic, can create a sound called 'popping'. It totally depends on your voice. If you're hearing little 'pops' when making these sounds, don't panic. You just might need to move the mic a bit further away. It's normal.

Why Do I need it?!

The microphone is your friend. There's a reason why it's there – it can make everything easier. Trust that. I have always found they've helped my nerves, but I totally recommend practising holding something. Mic in one hand, notes in the other. Recipe for success!

Without PA

It might be that you will not be using PA for a variety of reasons. You might have an aversion to it, or it won't be needed because the room is small. If this is the case, then some vocal health precautions and warmup exercises might be in order.

Gary Terzza's advice

I occasionally do voiceover work. When I first got started in that field, I was trained by the excellent coach and radio presenter Gary Terzza, who runs a service called Voiceover MasterClass. That was quite a long time ago, so I wanted to remind myself what Gary has to say on the subject of vocal health and warmups.

These tips come from a blog post Gary wrote for a

voiceover website called Voices.com. Although professional voiceovers are using their voices for much longer than a wedding speaker will ever need to, some of them might be helpful to you.

'We use it every day and yet the voice is one of the most neglected parts of our anatomy. Just think about how you use yours: chatting on the telephone, shouting at the kids, clearing your throat – the vocal cords endure a punishing schedule.

Of course if you use your voice professionally the demands are even greater; so how can you make sure you are giving this powerful but delicate organ the care and attention it deserves?

Take precautions to protect your voice

Don't misuse or abuse the larynx. Never smoke and keep away from smoky atmospheres. Keep shouting to a minimum. If you have a cold that's affecting the voice box, try and avoid talking. Dry dusty conditions, even air-conditioning, can dry out the voice significantly, so always take regular sips of water.

Try to reduce your caffeine intake as this can dry out the larynx and cause hoarseness. Equally watch your alcohol consumption as this not only has a physiological impact on your voice box, but reduces your inhibitions, making you more liable to raise your voice.

Make sure you do some warm up exercises. Gentle humming at a low level can help develop resonance, clear the airways and give those cords a soothing work-out, but be careful you don't strain.

Large meals can alter the tonal quality of your voice (ask any singer, or voice-over artist) and this is

especially true of spicy foods and dairy products.
For women, hormonal changes such as the menopause,
pregnancy or menstruation can have a marked effect
on the voice, as can stressful situations such as divorce
or bereavement. The voice is the articulator of emotion,
so tension or depression might show in your voice,
sometimes in quite unexpected ways.'

About the Author
Gary Terzza is a professional voiceover and coach
with a client list that includes Channel 4, Channel five,
VH-1 and the BBC. He also runs a voice-over master-
class in Central London and Hertfordshire.

Pete Judge's advice

I also consulted my friend Pete Judge. He's a brass player
and he also conducts a choir in which I sing, so he knows
a lot about breath control for both activities. Here are his
suggestions:

1. Physical warm-ups:
- lifting shoulders to ears, then releasing (repeat a few
times)
- rotating shoulders (& repeat in the other direction)
- shaking out the hands and arms, and feet and legs (8
shakes of right arm, 8 of left, 8 of right leg, 8 of left;
then 4 of each...2 of each...1 of each)
- gentle stretching exercises (nick some from a yoga
site?!)
- gentle neck & head exercises (very gentle rotations in
both directions)
- waking the face up: gentle rubbing with palms whilst
gurning...
- big mouth / little mouth (exaggerate!)

- breathing exercises ... not sure I know any good ones!
2. Vocal warm-ups:
- gentle rubbing of face with palms whilst starting to make soft noises
- gentle humming ... start on low notes ... try slurring between notes as well
- vocal slides (use one hand to 'conduct' yourself up and down)
- choose a note and elide between the vowel sounds ('AY-EE-I-O-OU')
- throwing sounds: use whole body and throw a single sound as far as you can with your hand, as if throwing a cricket ball (repeat)
- scribble with sounds (again, use the body)
- tongue-twisters on different consonant sounds:
"unique New York' / 'Debbie Blackett Peggy Babcock' / 'pa's got a head like a ping-pong ball' /
'Don't hold your hat in your hot hand, Harry: hang it on a hook in the hall' etc. etc.
- repeated consonant sounds: d, d, d, d,....t, t, t, t, ...k, k, k, k, ...m, m, m, m, ...n, n, n, n,.... 'ba da ga, pa ta ka' ...etc etc
- declaim sentences from your speech, aiming at different parts of the room (start by breathing in and declaiming for 10 seconds, then repeat for 15, then repeat for 20)'

Richard Burton ... and how he got that wonderful voice

Depending how old you are, you might or might not be aware of the talent of the legendary British actor Richard Burton. I say British; but if he were still alive he would probably insist on the fact he was Welsh. Moreover, his native tongue was Welsh and he couldn't speak a word of English until he went to school at the age of 5.

One of Burton's most recognisable attributes was his voice, which can still be enjoyed today; just Google his introduction to the opening of Dylan Thomas' famous BBC radio play *Under Milk Wood*, or his voiceover for the movie *War of the Worlds*.

How did he achieve that wonderful resonance? How much of his was nature and how much was nurture? By the way, Burton's real name was Richard Jenkins; he got his stage name from his secondary-school teacher. This man was a Welsh-born American, Philip Burton, who went on to become an acclaimed radio producer and theatre director. Burton (Philip) used to take Burton (Richard) walking on local hills and get him to declaim Shakespeare for hour upon hour.

That's fairly extreme and maybe you are not intending to become a famous actor. But it works! Here's a less extreme version: I used to coach a wedding speaker by taking him to a nearby beach and getting him to declaim his speech to me while standing some distance off, where he was competing with the sound of the wind and the waves.

'The beach exercise' is one that I learned from Cicero: indirectly of course, because sadly I never had the opportunity of meeting the man. That's how 'the greatest orator of the Roman Republic' was trained by his tutor when he was learning to be an advocate. If it was good enough for Cicero it's good enough for me.

Don't have a beach near you? Bad luck: but you can go anywhere in the open air where your voice has to compete with background noise, be it wind or traffic.

CHECKLIST

- ❑ If there is a PA system, have a dry run with it if possible on the morning of the big day.

- ❑ If there's no PA, have a look at the room before everything starts. Try out some phrases out loud. It won't sound the same when the room is full, of course; but it's still worth getting a feel for how your voice sounds.

- ❑ Read the voice warmup routines in this chapter. Decide which one you like. Do it several times when you're rehearsing and also (if you can find a quiet spot!) on the day.

Chapter 8

Time To Rehearse

'I am the most spontaneous speaker in the world, because every word, every gesture and every retort has been carefully rehearsed.'

George Bernard Shaw

So you've crafted a great speech. You've decided how to ensure you'll remember it. You've read my last chapter about the voice and about using PA. What's next? Embedding that speech and its delivery into your body, into the muscle memory as they say. How will you do that? Simple, but not easy: repetition, rehearsal. Repetition, rehearsal. And more rehearsal.

The Carnegie Hall

There's a famous story (well, famous in the United States, anyway) about a woman who was hurrying to a concert at New York City's legendary Carnegie Hall. She took a wrong turning, lost her way and asked a passer-by for directions. (That's how I know it was a woman: we guys would never ask for directions).

Here's the exchange:

'How do I get to Carnegie Hall?'

'Practise, lady. You gotta practise.'

OK, you aren't aiming to perform at Carnegie Hall; but this is equally important. One of the nicest compliments I've ever had was from someone I was coaching to speak at his daughter's wedding. Afterwards he wrote me the following testimonial: 'If you have to give the most important speech of your life, this is the man who can help you do it.' And one reason I treasure that compliment is that it came from a man in his mature years, who had been very successful in creating and running two substantial and totally different businesses. So it was definitely not the first speech of his life, but he considered it the most important.

It's important for you too. Therefore I echo the words of that passer-by in New York City ... 'you gotta practise'.

Cicero's rehearsal method

For years I've been a fan of Marcus Tullius Cicero, the Roman consul who was said to be the best orator in the Republic's history. He was only a name to me until I read Robert Harris's trilogy (*Imperium, Lustrum and Dictator*) about his life. Now I feel I know old Marcus Tullius (or Tully, as I call him: we're mates now) really well.

One story Harris tells about Cicero's early life has stayed with me for years. It's about 'training on a beach'. I believe it too, because although those books are classed as historical fiction, they've led me on to reading some of what we can call genuine historians writing at the time and later, from Livy to Suetonius to Gibbon, and on so many important points I've found the known facts support the skeleton on which Harris bases his story.

Anyway, I digress: I was talking about the beach. According to the legend, when Cicero was a young man and training to be an advocate, i.e. a lawyer, his father sent him to Greece to study with one of the most famous tutors of the day. This man used to take him to the beach where he had to practise (that word again) declaiming, so he could develop his voice projection sufficiently to be heard over the waves. After doing this for a long time, Cicero asked, 'When are we going to study **what** I should say, not **how** I should say it?' The tutor replied, 'In oratory, the three most important things are delivery, delivery and delivery.'

Now, you are not training to be a lawyer or in fact any kind of orator, and you could well have a PA system to help you, but there are lessons to be learned. Firstly, that rehearsing out loud, again and again, is important. Do it to the mirror, to a friend, to a partner, it doesn't matter. As Nike tells us, 'Just do it.' The other thing is that no matter how wonderful your words are, if they can't be heard then it's a waste. If you won't have a PA system on the day, then practise outside (and I now use this method when coaching speakers: there's a convenient beach not far from my home); but if you do have a PA, then refer to my section and microphone technique. Either way, refer also to my section on vocal warmups.

By the way, you might've noticed my story in an earlier chapter, about how the late great actor Richard Burton developed his famous voice. The principle is the same.

Pacing and pausing

One of the practical effects of the nerves of the occasion is that you will sometimes speak faster than you normally do. Be aware of this and compensate for it when you are rehearsing. If you aim to speak at about 150 words / minute, that's a good guideline.

Pausing between the main themes of your speech is a classy thing to do. What's more, it gives you a chance to catch your breath and your brain a chance to reorganise the remaining material. Finally, it gives your audience a chance to absorb what you've just said.

Pause for longer than seems natural to you: that's also because of the effect of adrenalin. The pause will not seem as long to the audience as it does to you.

Start and finish

How you start and how you finish are both very important, for several reasons. One of those reasons is to do with the audience. They are particularly likely to remember how you started and how you finished.

Another reason is to do with yourself. It's difficult to memorise the whole of a speech. Even if you can – and plenty of actors memorise a whole play, so you know it's possible with hard work – it is difficult to inject feeling into something you are saying by heart.

However, it's not hard to memorise the first few sentences and the last few sentences. That is what I urge you to do, whether or not you memorise the rest of your speech.

The bonus is this: if you know that you've memorised your opening few sentences and your closing few sentences, that will boost your overall confidence 100%.

How many rehearsals?

The man in New York said to the Carnegie Hall-seeking woman: 'you gotta practise'. How many times should you practise your speech, when you are finally happy with it? That's for you to decide. However, let me tell you about a singer-songwriter friend of mine, the wonderful Jim Reynolds. He's based in Bristol, in the West of England.

If you met him, and certainly if you saw him perform, you'd think he was the most laid-back man in the world. But Jim once told me that before he performs a new song, he rehearses it **forty to fifty** times.

Yes, he's a pro. But that's an example worth following.

CHECKLIST

- ❑ Make your first draft
- ❑ Make as many more drafts as you need
- ❑ Finalise your speech
- ❑ Print it out
- ❑ Read it in front of the mirror
- ❑ Repeat (Five times? Fifty times? You choose. See my story above)
- ❑ Run it through again a few times with a real audience: friend, partner, dog, cat.

Chapter 9

Confidence On The Day

'If you have stage fright, it never goes away. But then I wonder: is the key to that magical performance because of the fear?'

Stevie Nicks

So the big day has arrived. This is where I give you a last-minute pep-talk about how to capitalise on all the preparation you've done. And how to ensure you'll keep a clear head.

Like pretty well everyone else, I get nervous before speaking. That's despite the fact that I've been speaking in public for many years. If ever I stop getting nervous, I should probably stop speaking in public.

I know that a certain amount of nervous tension is essential to a good performance. But of course I need to control that tension. Those two facts are central to this book.

This is where I suggest that if you skipped Chapter 1, you go back and read it now.

Mental preparation

The methods I covered at the start of this book are most effective if they've been part of your preparation right from the time the wedding date was fixed. If you've done that, then they'll be the foundation of your confidence on the day. You're going to have a mental picture, or a word, or a physical gesture; whatever you chose, you'll utilise it to trigger the feeling, or mindset, that you want.

In Chapter 1 I talked about Muhammad Ali's so-called 'Future History' method, of creating a mental picture in advance of an event, picturing in detail the outcome you want and then carrying that mental picture around with you until the event happens. Practitioners of NLP (neurolinguistic programming) call it, I believe, a 'well-formed outcome'. It apparently worked for Ali, though he did have other advantages.

[By the way, if you're a science fiction reader, you'll know that *Future History* was also the title of a series of stories by the famous author Robert Heinlein. In fact, the Oxford English Dictionary's online version says: 'Future History (in science fiction) = a narration of imagined future events.' Not just science fiction, because it fits Muhammad Ali's use of the phrase perfectly.]

I then talked about another technique that's well known to NLP people; sometimes called 'the circle of excellence' and sometimes 'anchoring' (again, a disclaimer: I am not qualified in these matters). In that one, you are accessing the feeling you had in the past when you were in the state of mind that you want to be in when giving your speech; and creating a physical signal to yourself in order to access that feeling on demand. I've personally used that and found it very effective.

The third method I talked about was the 'safe place' method and maybe that one is the best of all if you are really very stressed out by the speaking challenge. It consists of imagining a place that you associate with feelings of calm and well-being (perhaps a beach that you've always liked) and deciding on a word that will be a signal to yourself that calls up the calming scene.

If you haven't read Chapter 1, please do so now. If you've already read it (as I said at the start, this is not a book that has to be read from start to finish in the correct order) then go back and skim it again regarding the techniques.

Then decide which of those techniques suits you best, and you'll have a tool to utilise during the intervening time, and also on the day.

Cutting out distractions

I mentioned that my younger daughter Madeleine is a professional actor. I once asked her about her routine preparing for a stage performance. The simplest thing, she said, was that for a couple of hours beforehand, she didn't want any unnecessary distractions. So she'll switch her phone off a long way ahead of 'curtain up' time. I know to send her those 'break a leg' text messages early in the day. It's basic but essential.

Last-minute routines and rituals: what do singers do?

Putting myself in your shoes: let's say I have done everything right so far: the broad-brush planning, the research if necessary, the drafting of the speech (and redrafting), the final version; preparation of my aides-memoire and then finally the rehearsal time. Underpinning all those activities, I have chosen a mental strategy to manage my brain between the wedding date being fixed and the actual day. Having done all that, is there anything else I should do at the last minute, or anyway in the last hour, to ensure that my head is in the right place before I start speaking?

A few years ago I was pondering this question and I wondered ... can I learn about last-minute routines and rituals from other types of performers, who also have to give their best performances at a specific and prearranged time? I believe I can.

I thought, for example, of athletes, of actors, of musicians.

To begin, I looked at music. I focused just on popular musicians, because (a) we know a lot about them and (b) Noel Coward was right when he said: 'It's extraordinary how potent cheap music is.' Half a dozen examples just within the genre of popular vocalists are worth thinking about.

- **Chris Martin** of Coldplay brushes his teeth, because, he says: 'otherwise I don't feel smart enough.'

- **Beyonce**'s contract calls for ten bottles of mineral water in her dressing room, which have all been opened long enough to have gone flat.

- **Stevie Nicks** of Fleetwood Mac has a shot of tequila. That raises the whole question of alcohol, which is a big part of most wedding celebrations in our culture. I have sung in a lot of choirs in my time and one of my fellow-singers once told me that she always has one drink before a performance 'just to take the edge off.' That makes sense to me; but sadly some wedding speakers feel that they have to get pretty drunk in order to handle the nerves of the occasion. That'll get rid of the nerves but will probably get rid of the chance of a good speech.

- **Robert Plant** of Led Zeppelin: in his dressing-room he used to drink a mug of tea, and iron his stage clothes, in order 'to get in the mood'. This behaviour by the possessor of that famous voice is 'not very rock-n-roll' but it clearly worked for him.

- The late great **Leonard Cohen** used to recite Latin chants with his backing singers; and he drank a whisky. Because of stage fright, in the past he had to drink three bottles of wine before performing. It then changed to 'just a whisky'; but I suspect it was probably a very large one.

… and finally …
- The late great **Elvis Presley** and 'the thousand-yard walk'. When he was playing a large arena, he would insist that his trailer was parked 1000 yards from the stage. That way, the last thing he would do before performing would be that solitary walk. (OK, not exactly solitary: he probably had one or two security men with him but there would be no conversation). That way his concentration would not be broken by distractions and he could keep his head 'in the zone.' By the time he got to the stage, his mindset would once again be that of 'The King.'

You don't have a trailer? No problem. Go for a walk

around the block!

Food and caffeine are common props and comfort sources when we're stressed; but we humans can survive without those for a long time. We can't last long without water or air. So arrive early, get set up, ensure there's water to hand for when you speak, then go for a walk around the block. That way you can benefit from Elvis's example.

You don't like Elvis? Choose a musician or actor or athlete you admire; learn what they do to prepare. Solomon said 3000 years ago: 'there's nothing new under the sun.' In this field, that's absolutely true; find your role model and learn.

It's definitely worth checking out some actors' warmup routines. We know that many famous actors – musicians too – throw up in the wings but I'm not suggesting that as a warmup ritual. The legendary Henry Fonda, who was still performing on the Broadway stage at the age of 75, would throw up in the wings before going on. If the great Henry Fonda was always nervous, what does it tell the rest of us?

Helga Weissmeiler of the University of Munich's Institute of Theatre Studies monitored several actors' pulse rates during rehearsals and performances, and found that they went as high as 175 per minute or more during monologues. Readings this high had previously been observed only in test pilots during takeoff and landing, she said.

Clearly this is a fascinating area, so if you're interested in theatre, then you might find it a worthwhile exercise to ask Google about the mental preparation strategies and last-minute rituals of actors. I suspect that the results of such a search will populate the second edition of this book.

'The demon drink'

One of my fellow-singers says she has just one drink before a performance 'to take the edge off'. It's a very common strategy. And many of the famous singers in the list you've just read use routines that include booze. Because drink is a part of most weddings in our culture, it's worth talking about this some more.

In the early stages of writing this book, I was working in a cafe. There were two thirty-something Brits at the next table, of an age when one goes to a lot of weddings. So I introduced myself and asked 'have you spoken at a wedding recently? And if so, how much did you drink beforehand?'

Both were pretty frank, although I was a total stranger. Maybe because I was a total stranger. One said 'five or six pints of beer, to take the edge off'. The other said 'I was so nervous; I couldn't face the task without getting wasted first.'

That was a random sample, although a very small one. And 100% of my small sample drank a lot before speaking. By contrast, I asked a client after he'd spoken at his daughter's wedding, 'How much did you drink before you spoke?' Admittedly, being the father of the bride, he was thirty years older than those two strangers in the cafe.

His answer: 'Just half a glass of wine. I'm a control freak. I wanted to get the speech right.'

We've all got different attitudes to alcohol and, importantly, different tolerances to it. Therefore, I have no intention of recommending what's a prudent amount to drink before speaking. However, you don't need to be a control freak to realise that you too want to get it right. Therefore, you'll decide how much is just enough, not too much. I can't tell you the amount; you'll know it.

By the way, that client and I had discussed booze previously. I suggested a strategy: because I knew he would limit his intake before speaking, maybe he would allow himself a reward when the speech was finished. So I said 'Why not put a large glass of your favourite drink visible in front of you, which you've decided you won't touch till you sit down again?' So that's what he did. A large whisky was therefore in view, to be enjoyed when he sat down.

CHECKLIST

- ❑ Referring back to Chapter 1, utilise the mental trigger you chose. Do it at least an hour before you speak.

- ❑ Switch your phone off at least an hour before you're going to speak! You don't want any distractions: remember Elvis Presley's '1000-yard walk'.

- ❑ Having picked your last-minute routine or ritual, do it during the last hour. Repeat your trigger word or image or action.

- ❑ Before you start speaking, make sure you have water to hand. If you don't, you might end up drinking more wine than you'd planned.

Chapter 10

Tips From The Professionals

'Many a good argument is ruined by some fool who knows what he is talking about.'
Marshall McLuhan

If you've read this far, you'll have learned that I have a lot of interest in the subject of wedding speeches. I've been to scores of weddings and spoken at many of them. But it's an occasional activity for me. So I thought it would be good (essential, in fact) to consult some of the many professionals who work in this field.

I visited wedding fairs and spoke to some of these professionals. I asked if they'd like to contribute to this book and here you have the result. These are the people who hear wedding speeches every week and as a result they represent 'the fool who knows what he's talking about.'

Giles Bracher. Photographer, Bristol and SW Spain

http://weddingsbygiles.com/
- 'Coordinate with the other speakers! I don't want

to hear the same story twice. Multiple best men are OK if they do it as a tag team but that requires planning.

- I hate speakers who don't know the rules and think it's OK to just stand there and chat.

- My worst experience: a groom who just read his speech from an iPad ... and it lasted an hour, despite dirty looks from the bride.

- Ideally each speech should last 5-10 minutes

- The current trend to spread the speeches out, e.g. in between courses, not all at the end of the meal, is to be welcomed.

- Always use PA! A stand mic is fine; one of the ushers can make sure it's at the right height for each speaker. Cautionary tale: if using a lapel mic (which presupposes that there's a sound engineer), be sure to switch it off if you go to the loo!'

Brigid Holdsworth. Venue host, Yorks

I have been a wedding host at a classy venue in Yorkshire (yes, we do have them) for five years and have sat through a few. I cannot remember the content exactly, just the general tone/theme, and a few stand out.

One family who obviously could not really afford to use the place, one overweight bride in shiny cream satin and one slightly weedy groom. His speech to her was so moving that we, and most of the guests were in tears. He looked straight at her as he spoke. Basically he told her why he loved her, how much she had done for him, how she made him a better man, how awful his life was before they met and how she made his life complete. It was wonderful and totally unexpected.

One couple, both looking very ill, spoke about the importance of transplant surgery! The bride clutched a huge box or medicines throughout the day. We were very nervous.

The most sickening was an 'older' bridegroom with far too many adoring friends. (I thought he was the bridegroom's father!) Each table was for a different group of friends, sports, cycling, work, family, motorbikes, Uni friends, etc. He had three best men, all of whom were inspired to speak at great length about his various amazing qualities, his escapades, his full and interesting sex life and his prowess at all sporting activities. The stunner was from the last best man, sixty minutes later, who told a joke in very bad taste, the punchline of which was 'well, you asked me to cook your sock'! The wedding guests were stunned into silence (but I do remember the joke!); there were older family members who luckily didn't get it. It was sickening as the new wife, a younger model than the previous forty-five-year-old, tried to keep herself in the picture by having a Best Woman speech and that went down like a lead balloon amongst his true fans. The speeches that time took two hours in total.

A recent wedding did not follow the traditional pattern, father of the bride, groom, then best man. The bride and groom stood side by side and told the story, taking turns, about how they met and what they loved about each other. So refreshing and mercifully short.

The father of the bride speeches are the dullest, tales of ballet lessons, and lots of success in everything they ever tackled. Not original, truthful or interesting. We had one best man who was very rude about the new wife; we were horrified ... did he really say that? In many instances one wonders why the best man isn't marrying the groom, the LOVE is palpable.

My nephew had us all in tears, not speeches to the crowd at all, the bride and groom spoke to each other about what they loved about each other, what they planned for the rest of their lives, how they intended to bring up their family, and their beliefs etc. They are still married after twenty years.

My brother-in-law, a very shy man, at his daughter's wedding stood up and said 'My job is to welcome you all and to thank you for coming, so welcome and thank you for coming.' He sat down. Perfect.

My advice, let the bride or best woman speak, to even-out the adoration, use a microphone, do not tell jokes at all, set a timer and KEEP IT SHORT!!

Martin Norsworthy. Photographer, Kingsbridge

https://www.norsworthyphotography.com/
During rehearsal I tell the speakers where to stand. That way they can address the guests while still being seen by me. The answers to this depend partly on the table arrangements, i.e. is there a top table or will the main players be sitting at one of the round tables?

Polly Tisdall. Professional storyteller, Bristol

http://www.pollytisdall.com/
Polly's Worst Crimes:

- Speaking for too long.
- Not consulting the other speakers.
- Lack of personal context to stories.

Polly's Top Tip:
Think about how you want to make your audience feel: what do you want to leave them with? (Maya Angelou again!)

Tasha Park. Photographer, Bristol

https://tashapark.co.uk/
Keep it short and sweet – even the best speeches become difficult to listen to past the 15 minute mark.

Try using props & making it interactive – I shot a wedding recently where the best man did a wonderful speech using props. He brought along a 'Pie Face Game' (check it out on YouTube!) and every time the groom was mentioned the crowd had to shout his name and he had to play this Russian Roulette-style game. It involved the audience and made them laugh (innocently) at the groom's expense. The best man also brought a pen along and told us that he was going to use it to help himself not to cry – he would click it whenever he felt tearful.

Another best man brought along an actual bucket of KFC and a 3 foot blow up mobile phone to illustrate some of the groom's character traits – this was so bizarre having just had the wedding meal that it was hilarious, but a very simple crutch.

Keep it clean! Weddings are strange beasties as it's a mix of your friends and family and they have to all be entertained. The best way to get laughs out of your stag do is probably not the same way to get a gentle chuckle out of your Grandma. Silly comedy and a bit of lewdness can be fun but no swearing or vomiting stories please.

Keep it relevant – I once listened to a forty-minute Father of the Bride speech where he began talking about the bride and her strength as a woman in a man's world. All very lovely to begin with, but then he kept with the subject for another twenty mins, no longer talking about the bride but about the plight of women in Saudi Arabia. All very important stuff but not to take up time on your daughter's wedding day. This one day is all about her.

Don't read from a card or notes if at all possible and keep it conversational – tone of voice and eye contact is really important. One guy I saw read his whole speech from a smartphone in a monotone and it wasn't at all captivating.

Don't RUSH – look around, smile, laugh along with your audience.

Prof. Malcom Heggie. Academic (and standup-in-training)

Malcolm Heggie is a professional for sure, but he would never describe himself as a wedding professional. He's a chemistry professor at a British university; a very pleasant bloke I met on a train once. What made him especially interesting from my point of view (apart from the fact that I'd studied chemistry at university, albeit to less successful effect) is that he belongs to something pretty unique called the Bright Club. At their meetings, academics in a variety of fields polish their public speaking skills by the very scary method of delivering stand-up routines to their peers, from whom they then get feedback.

Malcolm gave some great advice to his younger brother Douglas, then preparing to speak at his elder daughter's wedding. It's so good that I wish I had remembered it when I was about to perform the same task.

Here's Malcolm's top tip for the father of the bride:

'Just before the meal, while people are finding their places and sitting down, go round the tables "glad-handing" everyone you already know. That contact will do a lot to steady your nerves.'

Phil McCheyne. Photographer (retd), balloon pilot

https://twitter.com/McCheynePhil

One of my bridegrooms bent down to tie a shoelace and split his trousers. An indication of Murphy's Law: if something can go wrong, it might go wrong. Be prepared!

On the same topic: we photographers always carry at least one spare camera. What's your backup plan if you're a speaker?

Sharon Stiles. Hypnotherapist, Bristol & online

www.sharonstiles.co.uk/

These days (Michael speaking) I live in Bristol, which is the most amazingly creative city. When I moved here, I made more new friends in the first three months than I had made in the preceding 10 or 15 years living in smaller places.

One of those friends is a hypnotherapist. Her name is Sharon Stiles and she is a great communicator. I recently met up with her and she told me that she sometimes consults people who are about to speak in public and are terrified at the prospect. She even has a self-hypnosis audio available on her website, specifically for the best man at a wedding.

Some people would see this as a last resort but it is a better alternative than the common strategy of getting drunk first, or taking a Valium or similar.

Here's what Sharon says on the subject.

Hypnosis has three elements to it. A suggestion, belief in that suggestion and then repetition of that suggestion. If you are anxious about something then you are actually using a form of hypnosis – just not with the most helpful outcome. However, the good news is that if you can create anxiety then hypnosis is likely to work well for you. All the hypnotherapist needs to do is to give you more positive suggestions that you can believe.

There are a variety of ways to achieve the state of mind where hypnosis is effective. The most common method is to use relaxation. When you are relaxed your mind is calmer and so is more open to accepting new ideas, alternative possibilities and listening to your rational thoughts. If you find it difficult to relax, don't worry, there are other hypnosis techniques that can be used instead.

The easiest way to describe hypnosis to someone who hasn't been hypnotised is that it is similar to daydreaming. You are aware of what is happening but your mind might drift off and you become lost in your thoughts.

For some situations a hypnotherapy track may be sufficient. They can be an effective and low-cost way to give yourself positive suggestions and reinforcement for thinking a specific way.

If you have a lot of anxiety, the suggestions on the hypnosis track don't seem relevant to you or they simply aren't working for you then I would recommend seeing a hypnotherapist. A personalised session will be related to your specific needs and can address your own personal situation.

What happens as part of a hypnotherapy session will vary, depending on the hypnotherapist. Some will purely give you positive suggestions that describe the way you would like things to be. Others will address events from the past that might be related to what you want to change.

If you would like to use a hypnotherapist to help to reduce anxiety about public speaking then make sure that you find one you feel comfortable with. Ask friends if they have any recommendations. Read websites and pick someone who you feel you can relate to. That is really important because if you don't feel the person understands you or isn't listening to you then you are less likely to allow the suggestions to work for you. Hypnosis is a partnership between hypnotist and hypnotee. It isn't a case of the hypnotist telling the hypnotee what to do.

My top tips are:

Keep a balanced view of the speech

Our minds store up memories of actual experiences and also store our imagined experiences. This means that if you keep thinking about things going badly your mind will expect that to happen. Your experience is that you have given your wedding speech hundreds of times before you've even got to the wedding day and each time it wasn't a good experience.

'Bring some balance in by spending time imagining the speech going well. Hear your voice, strong and calm, giving the speech you have prepared so well. See the smiles around the room and hear the guests laughing at the right points. Allow yourself to enjoy it.

'Now, your mind has an experience of the speech going well that it can draw on next time you think about the wedding. This allows you to feel calmer and give a much better speech.

Rub your wrist

If you feel panicky and overwhelmed, perhaps with a blank mind, use this technique. You can usually do this without anyone noticing what you are doing. There is an acupressure point on the inside of your wrist (where a wristwatch would be). Use two fingers of your other hand to rub very gently in a circle on this point and simply focus your attention on doing that. After a while you will probably take a slightly deeper breath and feel calmer.

Bad experiences

I have been at a couple of weddings of friends where the best man was extremely nervous about giving his speech. On both occasions the best man used alcohol to try and calm his nerves and on both occasions the speech suffered because of it with parts of the speech being given at the wrong points, people's names forgotten and the best man becoming more and more embarrassed.

Although it was a bad experience for those men, it

didn't ruin anyone else's day (please remember that if anything goes wrong in your speech!). I just wish I had known about their anxiety before they hit the bottle so that I could have helped them to calm their nerves in a more effective way.

YOUR TIMELINE

To conclude, a reminder of one of my mottos: 'it's never too soon to begin planning a speech.' With that in mind, here's a timeline that you might find it helpful to follow. Most of these steps have already appeared elsewhere in this book.

Good luck!

Step	Target date	Done?
Mental preparation: creating a picture of your desired outcome.		☐
Broad-brush planning: deciding the structure. (The Foolscap Manifesto?)		☐
Researching for stories		☐
Creating a skeleton of what you're going to say		☐
Writing your first few sentences and your last few sentences		☐
Writing your first draft		☐
Completing the final text		☐
Preparing aides-memoire		☐
Rehearsing		☐
More rehearsing!		☐
Switching off your phone (at least an hour before speaking)		☐
Making sure you have plenty of water to hand		☐

Step	Target date	Done?
Utilising the mental trigger you chose previously		☐
Doing any last-minute ritual you chose		☐
Repeating your trigger word or image or action		☐
Taking three deep breaths		☐
Delivering a wonderful speech!		☐

RESOURCES

Link to the book *Public Speaking for Authors, Creatives and Other Introverts* by Joanna Penn (see my Chapter 4 for an authorised extract): https://amzn.to/2JFbh4K .

Find all Joanna Penn's books, plus her blog and podcast, at www.TheCreativePenn.com

DID YOU ENJOY THIS BOOK?
DID YOU FIND IT HELPFUL?

If yes, hopefully to both questions, then I'd really appreciate it if you could post a review on Amazon or Goodreads. Recommendations from other readers – social proof, as some people call it nowadays – are really valuable to writers.

OTHER EDITIONS AND SERVICES

Other editions of this book are planned, including print and audio versions. I also offer 1:1 coaching for speakers at weddings and other events, whether social or professional.

MAILING LIST

If you'd like to hear from me (occasionally!) about my future projects, there's a signup form on my website. Here's a link to the home page where you'll find it: www.michaelmacmahon.com

ABOUT THE AUTHOR

Michael MacMahon was born in Pembrokeshire and educated at St George's College, Weybridge and Imperial College, London. He spent most of his career in the chemical industry and then worked in media relations for a health-sector charity. In between those phases, he set up and ran a training consultancy.

Nowadays, when not writing, he's a coach; he specialises in helping nervous speakers and also people contemplating retirement or considering reinvention. He's an occasional voice actor, broadcaster and speaker, who lives in Bristol and looks forward to his next phase.

ACKNOWLEDGEMENTS

This book and its author owe a debt of gratitude to many friends, acquaintances and family members without whose ideas, support and advice it would have been started – I'm good at that – but never finished. With apologies to anyone I have forgotten, their names are:

Alan Steel
Alison Donaldson
Brigid Holdsworth
Caroline Kataria
Chris MacMahon
Dan Holloway
Danny Kataria
Debbie Young
Ed Daniels
Gary Terzza
Geoff Haslam
Giles Bracher
Jackie Hawken
Jackie MacMahon
Jane Steward
Jim Reynolds
Joanna Penn

John Lynch
Ken Wydro
Kyla Rhind
Madeleine MacMahon
Malcolm Heggie
Martin Norsworthy
Paul MacMahon
Paul Taylor
Pete Dalby
Pete Judge
Phil McCheyne
Polly Tisdall
Rosalind Minett
Sharon Stiles
Stephen Bacon
Steve Roberts
Susan Dugdale
Tasha Park
Tess Biddington
Tim Arnold
Tom Walker

And special thanks to my professional supporters, who have 'gone the extra mile' to ensure that this book would be published.
Cartoons by David Lewis: http://davidlewiscartoons.com/
Coaching and generally keeping me on track by Jacqui Lofthouse: http://thewritingcoach.co.uk/
Cover design by Jessica Bell: http://www.jessicabellauthor.com/book-cover-design-services.html
Editing by Lin White: http://www.coinlea.co.uk/

Printed in Great Britain
by Amazon